Sibling of an Alcoholic

Sibling of an Alcoholic

Who Stole My Voice

ANNAY AUTH

RESOURCE *Publications* · Eugene, Oregon

SIBLING OF AN ALCOHOLIC
Who Stole My Voice

Resource Publications
An Imprint of Wipf and Stock Publishers
199 W. 8th Ave., Suite 3
Eugene, OR 97401

www.wipfandstock.com

PAPERBACK ISBN: 979-8-3852-5376-0
HARDCOVER ISBN: 979-8-3852-5377-7
EBOOK ISBN: 979-8-3852-5378-4

VERSION NUMBER 08/22/25

Contents

Preface

If you thought the title was a little bland, you are completely correct. However, when I was in the midst of everything, I wanted to know that someone understood what I was going through and validation that I wasn't crazy. I wasn't sure where to begin looking so I ended up typing "sibling of an alcoholic" into Google and couldn't find any books. This is for the next person who needs to know someone else understands the chaos and heartbreak they are facing while they watch their siblings slowly kill themselves with alcohol.

While writing this, I can't count the number of times I was told that "it wasn't my story" or that "I had to be the bigger person because I was healthy." But at the end of the day, I am writing about how addiction has impacted my life. I deleted portions that I felt were not mine to share, but for siblings of alcoholics, it deeply imprints on every aspect of our lives, and as a result, addiction becomes ingrained into each of our unique stories whether we consume the substance or not.

Introduction

Addiction. It's crazy how such a simple word can be so devastating and so life altering. It's also crazy how resources are abundant for addicts as well as parents and children of addicts, yet none for siblings. I guess people assume that since we're a bit older and able to distance ourselves, it shouldn't affect us as much as everyone else. I don't know, maybe it doesn't affect me as much as others, but it deeply impacts every part of my life. It influences my focus, my compassion, my trust, and my safety.

I want people to read this and feel supported, like they have a companion through the chaos. I want outsiders to get a taste of what it's like so they can support their friends. It's hard to start a book because pinpointing one specific moment as the beginning of addiction is nearly impossible. Even when we think of the start, with hindsight, we begin to see the hidden details that were so easily overlooked previously. I will attempt to break this up into different chapters focused on different emotions, but separating one feeling from another is something I struggle with. There seems to be a whiplash of emotions constantly swirling around my mind. One second there's happiness because you're having a family get-together and it's been ages since you caught up with everyone. Minutes later everything has flipped upside down and there's a drunken tantrum that changes all plans for the rest of the night. For families of addicts, this is completely normal, and you learn how to adapt to the screaming and threats. We pretend it's normal because normal has lost all meaning, but then again so have most words. So, in the setting of words no longer fitting their definitions, I will do my best to explain my journey and lessons as a sibling of an alcoholic.

I couldn't think of any way to be more authentic than sharing journal entries from when I was going through some of the trials. Some of the entries might be a little confusing or seem like a spiral of thoughts, but it would be a lie to make it seem like my mind was clear or that my life was making sense. I made mistakes and acted poorly as you will see from my thoughts and actions. There are times that I'm not proud of my behavior, but I can't rewrite history any more than I can eliminate addiction from my sister's life.

Throughout this book, it's so important to personalize my sister. I don't want anyone to think of Amber as an item that can be objectified. In many ways, it would be easier if she was a villain and we didn't share so much history. However, she's not a stranger. She's someone who has been ingrained into every aspect of my life. I have so many amazing memories with her and never want her to be seen as a horrible person. One of the hardest aspects of addiction is that the person causing you so much heartache is a loved one. I couldn't figure out how to personalize Amber in any way that represents how truly amazing, strong, loving, supportive, and protective she was to me growing up. The only compromise I could think of was to add short stories at the beginning of each chapter to always remember that addiction isn't the sole descriptor of who Amber is.

1

Reality

SHORT STORY

As kids, Amber and I would spend hours searching for fairies. We would make believe that each nub of a tree and every cloud in the sky represented a different village or fairy colony. We would create entire stories for the fairies down to their outfits and families. We did a similar thing with paper dolls. I can't count the number of hours we spent making up fake lives and stories for each character. We were so good at creating false realities and new adventures through our imaginations. To this day, I don't get bored because there's always something in my mind or a story that I can replay to keep me entertained. My current reality tends to feel fictitious because of how peculiar things are. At these times, I like to go back to my fairy-finding days and live in those moments while remembering who my sister truly is at her core.

SUMMARY

I very rarely share any of my family secrets, but the few times I do tell someone that my sister is an addict, I always feel like it isn't quite deep enough. One sentence doesn't sum up the anxiety of waiting on a call that is yet to come, telling me she finally overdosed or drank herself past where she could wake up. One word doesn't do justice to the heartbreak of watching your family's hearts shatter and hoping they don't fall for her lies. You can't fully define what it feels like to have ER visits be a part of daily life. It means never being able to feel safe because, at any time, your sibling might come in and start having a tantrum or begin terrorizing the room. It's these moments that you can't explain to anyone because the words just don't make sense. The sentences won't form just right or do justice to the feelings you have.

JOURNALS

Journal Entry 1

Amber is throwing tantrums, drinking, and will definitely try something tonight. Dad says he will go check on her throughout the night. I didn't ask to verify, but I can only assume it's to make sure she stays alive until morning. What a weird reality this life is. I keep thinking I can get used to it, but it's constantly one thing after another. Blow after blow of messy, gooey life.

Journal Entry 2

Mom just told me she tracks Amber's phone to see where she stops to drink on the way home. I guess she has a spot a mile from the house that she stops at so that she can get drunk before she gets home. Apparently mom confronted her about it. Amber thought she would be proud because she wasn't drinking and driving very far. . . . Is this the bar we've set, where it's a victory if she only drives a mile or two drunk? Also, if she has control over it, then why is she an alcoholic? If she has control over when/where she wants to drink, then why can't she hold off on drinking for longer? I don't want my life to revolve around her and, unfortunately, everything in this house does, so when I'm in the house I'm involuntarily picked up and flipped around with it.

Journal Entry 3

I used to want to know specifics and question every last detail of situations. However, with this experience, I've learned that I want to know as little as possible. I dread details and hate learning new information. My stomach sinks with the yelling. My breath retracts with each outburst that I try to ignore.

The most recent situation was Dad calling Mom and me on our way home to tell us we were walking into a bombshell. Amber was giving the ultimatum of, either she was allowed to drink or she would kill herself. I have no words other than what a strange life I live. I'm in my room listening to Amber scream at Mom while she scrambles through her room to get rid of the leftover alcohol. My abs are in a constant state of retraction as I flinch with every thud and scream. Tonight is the kind of night I lock the doors and hope everyone wakes up in the morning.

Journal Entry 4

I feel like I'm in a dream or acting in a play. There's no way this is my actual life. Amber had an alcohol-induced psychotic break and spent the day in the ER. I was told they couldn't force her to do a drug or alcohol screen and she refused them. This sounds questionable, but I've stopped asking questions. The hospital offered a seventy-two-hour hold, but my parents decided to let her sober up at home. Her counselor was there and talked to my parents about a treatment center in Dallas. Maybe it's good that Mom and Dad are starting to realize the severity of the situation, believing that my thoughts aren't completely crazy when I talk about Amber needing help. Then again, there's a piece of me that has been holding onto my parents' sweet oblivion and hoping I was being dramatic through this all.

I wonder if this is what a coma feels like, trying to wake up for a year. Feeling like everything has changed yet nothing is different all at the same time.

Journal Entry 5

I don't know how to share my experiences and life without being sappy or pessimistic. I was hiking with a friend and talking about Christmas traditions and how fun it was to share those things with family. A part of me loved reminiscing about the things we do and the memories I've had, but at the front of my mind was how my sister got hammered last Christmas Eve. How she threw a tantrum in the middle of presents and it totally killed the vibe. How she determined every event we did because of her manipulation and drinking. Even worse for me is realizing that this year will be no different unless she kills herself or someone else first.

Journal Entry 6

I'm pretty sure I ask this daily now, but once again I'm sitting here wondering, How did my life get so messed up? How is this normal? I want to cry every time I explain my reality to others. I don't know how to share or deal with the mundane idiocies of other people's daily lives when my world is constantly being flipped upside down.

Apparently Amber has been staying in a hotel the past few nights because she didn't want to deal with my parents. She also didn't show up to work today . . . how my parents know that I'm not sure, but I'm flooded with a mixture of emotions. Part of me is hopeful that I could have a somewhat normal Christmas. . . . Fat chance of that, even if she's not there my parents will be forlorn and everything will be about mourning her absence. If she does grace us with her presence, our time will be filled with tantrums and drunk rages. I can't deal with it, I just can't.

I also have this sinking feeling like never before, like maybe this might be it. I think she might not wake up tomorrow, will I ever see my sister again?

Journal Entry 7

I received a phone call from my brother giving me a heads-up that Amber was getting recommitted to the hospital. I guess I could be in shock, but, honestly, hearing the news didn't feel like it was affecting me. There's always a small voice telling me that the branching effects will reach far into my life, like not being able to have my parents for a few weeks and going through the same issues of manipulation when she gets out and reacts to the real world again. But for one night, it's relieving to not have to worry about her safety.

I found out later that Amber tried to cut her wrists with a box cutter at work. They tried to get her committed but her blood alcohol was 0.39 and the behavior unit won't commit people until their levels are below 0.15 so they had to kill time before booking her a room. It blows my mind that her level was that high more than two hours after having her last drink. Do I want to know what the maximum level was?

Time seems to slow with big jolts of news. About twenty minutes after my brother's call, I could feel the dread seeping into me. It's like the dramatic events are needles that inject me. At first, the effect is unnoticed, but slowly the venom delves through my body and takes over my being. It disrupts my focus, inhibits my thoughts, and frustrates my emotions. One part of me is slowly processing this new event that has been incorporated into my life while the rest of my life is continuing as normal. I go to school, church, activities, etc., and part of me is there, but part of me is floating away from the devastation of my reality.

It's two hours later when I realize I'm definitely affected. Impacted in a very different way than before, yet hurting all the same. While I'm not crying and feeling guilt-ridden, I am distracted. I've flipped through three different Netflix shows because none of them have been able to grab my attention. I've done a million little things because I can't stay zoned into one actual event. I cooked blueberry muffins and tacos even though my appetite vanished with the phone call. So maybe this is progress, but I think it's more just a spiraling cycle. I hate that she holds this much control over me, and I'm sad my parents must once again deal with it while I'm simultaneously hopeful that they will finally realize the issues they've been denying. I'm also mad that they still are protecting her and not making her take responsibility. They continue to enable, and I continue to mourn the loss of them all.

It's easy to be hard on myself. I think my thoughts and emotions are either invalid or mean. After all, how could I judge someone who is sick? How could I be mad that the attention won't be on me when comparatively my life is quite literally more stable and healthier than hers? I know it might seem conceited or focused on unimportant things, but really, it's just hard to realize life will never be about you. Life is a conglomeration of single moments and group memories. It would be weird if someone's life was focused only on him or her, we would immediately see an issue with this. So then why do people not understand that it's just as weird to not have any of these moments focused on you?

Journal Entry 8

I'm struck by the irony of Amber ending up in a mental hospital due to a suicide attempt with superficial wounds that barely broke the skin and would have healed on their own. However, this same hospital cannot force her to be admitted for drinking, which undoubtedly will kill her if given enough time. The blood alcohol level she had today was high enough to cause sudden death. How is that not enough of a reason to admit her?

I've realized the sad truth before, but today I can't stop thinking about how infuriating the whole system is. The addict won't want help until they are getting help, but they have to want the help to get it. What a messed-up cycle. But then again, maybe that's the point. Maybe it reinforces the fact that it must be the addict wanting help. It doesn't matter how many of us give everything to them, they will continue to use their substances. In their minds, substance > family. It's not meant to be personal, it's simply a fact. In some ways, it's my fault that I choose to take it personally. The sooner I can realize that, the easier their actions are to accept as simply hurtful and not personally vindictive. Maybe the people who set up the system do know better than me, and they realized that no one would obtain the help offered until they were ready. As a result, a system was designed to reflect that. On the other hand, it's possible that whoever designed the system never had a loved one suffering from substance abuse and truly did create a broken system. I'll probably never know, but hopefully I'll at least be able to help change it in the future for the better.

Journal Entry 9

We just went through one of Amber's rooms. We found three huge wine bottles, one single-serve alcohol, and three cartons of empty wine boxes. Apparently, this is all from the past couple of days since the time Mom last cleaned out the room. While we were up there, Mom casually mentioned that she told dad if Amber kept living there, she was going to move out until Amber was gone. She even has a plan to live in one of their rental properties.

This is matter-of-fact information from Mom, so I know she doesn't realize my world just got rocked. How do I go back downstairs and smile, make small talk, and pretend like my life didn't just totally change? I can't imagine my parents living apart. Will my dad choose my sister over my mom? I think it had to come to this, but I don't even have words to express how I feel.

I'm worried about the stress and extra work my parents have had to take on. I'm sad that this is our reality. I'm exhausted from dealing with this. I'm hurt and in pain from all of it. I'm alone in what I'm thinking.

Journal Entry 10

Guess what? My family is once again getting torn to shreds. I've been watching a TV show called *Life Sentence*[1] and the main character lived in oblivion when she had cancer because everyone hid the truth from her. Then, once she was cured, she found out about all the chaos going on around her. I think I've had a break from the drama since I've been distracted by school, but now that I have a week of vacation it all starts back up.

Journal Entry 11

Amber just called me for the first time in eight months and told me that she tried to kill herself because of me. Logically, I know it's not true. I could tell by all the slurring and mismatched information that she was drunk when she called. I just don't know how to deal with my sister telling me she would kill herself because of me. I've tried so hard to lovingly detach, but I don't know how to let the words she says hurt less.

I saw an incoming call from Amber, and I knew I shouldn't have answered. But I simultaneously had this feeling that she may kill herself since the other times she has called have been to tell me, "I'm going to kill myself tonight unless you talk me out of it." I didn't want to regret not answering and live my life wondering what she would have said if she had taken her life. So, I answered, and she started by talking about how she decided she was bipolar and was going to get help the next day. She was slurring and kept repeating contradictory statements. I started to get annoyed as she continued to say opposing things and lie about half of the conversation. But then, as always, she pulled the sister card of "You're the only one I wanted to tell about this." After so much time apart, I truly was glad and still had some hope of getting my sister back.

The rest of the conversation destroyed any hope that was building up and cut directly into my heart. She pulled a fast 180° and switched to her angry persona: "It is your fault for not texting

1. Cardillo and Keith, *Life Sentence*.

me or keeping in contact." I reminded her that phones go both ways. She brought up that she had tried to kill herself and I didn't reach out. She then asked if I had any idea how much it hurt for me not to reach out when she tried to kill herself. She put it on me and, luckily, I was able to say how I felt. I told her she didn't know how it felt for me to know my sister tried to kill herself. She didn't know how it felt to have our mom call crying, and to not get to have time with our dad because he's so busy with her. She kept saying how much I had hurt her, so I eventually stood up for myself and told her she couldn't blame everything on me. Her response was repetitively telling me, "This is on you, me trying to kill myself is on you." I think I should be proud of myself for standing up for myself. I've never been able to voice how I feel so I guess I should see this as a victory. But I'm too devastated. My heart is shattered, I can't fathom anything more painful to be told. I know logically it's just the alcohol speaking, but I'm not good enough at compartmentalizing to let it not affect me. I'm in physical pain. I thought I would be done crying over her, but she continually finds ways to hurt me.

What if I can never forgive Amber? I don't want to be impacted. Unfortunately, I so, so am. I fell right into her scheme when she called, I missed having a sister so much that I was willing to overlook the unmistakable lies she was telling and ignore the fact that she was obviously drunk. I was willing to do all of that, and then it turns out all she wanted was to be able to blame me for everything. *I think I'm as disappointed as I am proud of myself.* In addition, I'm distraught at how much power she has to hurt me. I want to take that power away. I don't want her to control my life. As ironic as the timing is, I think I actually really do love Amber. I think I would be able to separate myself more and be unaffected if I didn't care so much about her. For the first time, I wish I didn't care about her . . . I've been so worried that I didn't love her, when, in fact, love is what caused all of this, gosh darn it.

I called Mom and Dad after the call because some part of my inner child desired comfort from them and someone to tell me that it wasn't my fault. They were distraught because Amber had not contacted them in three days. I understand logically that their mental capacity has been reached, but the only focus they had for the conversation was to get clues on where Amber might be and if she was okay. My heart was shattered figuratively, but Amber's liver might burst literally so that takes priority.

Journal Entry 12

O Lord my God, my soul is so downcast. Smiling feels exhausting. My heart aches with the pains of unknowing longings of what might come. Spinning thoughts surround me and impending doom lurks right ahead. I don't know if it's better or worse that I'm incapable of impacting outcomes. I have no control or voice over Amber going to rehab. I can't quiet the pounding voice in my head reminding me that many addicts die leaving recovery due to an overdose. That voice stills the whisper of hope that I long to trust. Hope. I say it's there, but how much do I actually contain and how much is it just casually listed as one of any number of outcomes to make sure bases are covered?

Journal Entry 13

Is it weird that Amber drinking Listerine to get drunk doesn't shock me? I guess there's a low alcohol content so it's a trick that many alcoholics use when resources are limited. It rocked my mom's world and I guess she was concerned about telling me. The reality is, I'm not even surprised. A little grossed out, but my opinion of her hasn't changed one drop. I'm not entirely sure what to make of that.

Journal Entry 14

I wonder if PTSD is contagious. I just had the funniest thought . . . My sister got PTSD, which exacerbated her drinking, which has affected my life so much that I have symptoms and issues with PTSD. The irony is amazing. A normal person would probably read this and think I'm certifiably insane, but when life is as tough as it currently is, you have to find quirky tidbits and shiny thoughts if you have any intention of retaining your ability to smile. You can either choose to laugh or you are guaranteed to cry. I would prefer the former, but there are definitely days I choose the latter. It's all about balance, right? At this point, it may be more about survival and trying to limit the impact of these events on my lifelong health. Potato/tomato or whatever people say.

Journal Entry 15

I needed a place to get away and change my focus, so I went to the zoo. A place where I wouldn't have to smile or pretend to be okay. A place where I wouldn't have to converse and pretend to care about anything else. While everyone else was there taking pictures and trying to create a day to remember, I was there trying to get to a place where I could finally forget everything going on in my life. I was almost there, I looked at the giraffes and their majestic movements. I stared at the huge elephants who blocked out everything else. I looked at zebras and went to a magical world. But then I got a text from my former boss asking me to fill out a survey. It's the smallest thing that shouldn't even affect a fly, but it was enough to ruin my façade for the day. I guess in reality it didn't ruin the day. My day was ruined hours ago when I heard the news that my sister tried to kill herself again. I can pretend and try to escape all I want, but the truth is, this is my life and it's really messed up. I don't know how to live this life, but that doesn't matter, what matters are the facts, and those unfortunately mean I'm stuck with this reality.

I ended up spending twenty minutes at some exotic monkey-like creature exhibit. There was a mom creature that had a baby who was six months old (according to the sign.) No matter what the baby did, the mom wouldn't let go of her hand. The baby would try to climb the ropes and jump in trees, but without fail, the mom would hold her back. There was another one of these creatures in the pen and whenever it would get close the mom would move herself and the baby away. She may know what's best for the baby, but maybe the baby needs to learn the hard way sometimes. Sure, there will be scrapes and bruises when you fly solo, but you can only go so far staying attached. I think it has been hard for me to understand how hard things are in Texas because I only see things from a distance. Anytime things get close, they disappear, making it easy for me to live in oblivion until yet another catastrophe hits. There are probably a lot of other lessons God could teach me if I would open my eyes and pay attention to the world around me.

"I know there's a reason for everything, even tiny raindrops."—Me

Journal Entry 16

Amber was released from the hospital today. I didn't want it to affect me, after all, this is routine at this point. I feel like it shouldn't impact me, yet it still does. All the fears, thoughts, and realities crash into me as my peaceful illusion of the past eleven days is ruined. My frustration and anger return as my parents are already back to enabling and have made zero changes to encourage a different outcome. I'm full of rage, fear, and sadness. I have incredible friends who put up with my crazy mood swings and instead of getting angry ask if I'm okay. I truly don't know what I'd do without them . . . something that bothers me is all the little triggers that constantly come out of nowhere. For example, as I wrote the word "truly" I wanted to change it. It's a word my sister always uses when she's drunk and trying to seem sincere or make up after causing an explosive disaster the night before. I cringe at the appearance of the word and all it represents. I thought things were starting to feel okay again, but it was just because she was in the hospital. That may be the most depressing thought of all.

2

Guilt

SHORT STORY

I can't count the times growing up that my brother and I would put fake spiders and frogs in my sister's bed. Amber and I shared a room, so it was perfect for pranks and being able to observe the aftermath. I don't know why we did it, I think it was because my brother and I loved creatures, while Amber was terrified of them. Also, we went to bed in order of age. I had to be in bed earlier than Amber and I would always be furious that I couldn't stay up and hang out with the family, just to be woken up every time Amber would come to bed. It was almost like a little piece of vindication that I could irritate my sister, as well as my parents, when she would go to bed. There's a piece of me that looks back even on these small times and wonders if I forced Amber to start coping instead of trusting me. What if I had been kind and she trusted me as a safe person? Could she have turned to me instead of substances?

SUMMARY

Guilt comes in so many forms. There's the guilt of wondering how you could be so oblivious and not realize everything being told to you was a lie. You can look back and see that your loved one's complete identity was a façade she didn't feel safe sharing with you. How is it possible to be so completely blind to someone directly in front of you? Furthermore, the self-blame is all too real. Wondering how I could have loved her better, questioning what could be so wrong with me that my sister needed to create a false identity.

Then there's the guilt over what might happen in the future. You begin to think through all the horrible things that addiction might cause. Constant terror about the families your addict may potentially destroy by driving drunk. Future guilt about events that you can't predict and fear that you aren't doing enough to stop them.

Lastly, you start to feel guilty about living your own life when addiction has been happening for years. There are so many times when I hear about suicide threats or a hospitalization, and my new gut reaction has become hope that it doesn't mess up the plans I already have in place. If this was me a few years ago, I would be horrified at how callous that sounds, but it's so frequent that you become numb to things. However, there's still that tiny piece of your brain that continues to remind you throughout your plans with friends that you're putting your family on the back burner. That brings guilt back to center stage.

JOURNALS

Journal Entry 1

I hope Amber doesn't hurt or kill anyone; I can't imagine living with knowing she destroyed a family's Christmas forever. I've done all I can do by sending a letter to the cops sharing my concerns. If I see anything while I'm visiting my parents' house or know that she's leaving drunk, I'll have to call 9-1-1. Easier said than done, it's much easier to talk "the talk" about things. I've been able to forget and live life this week. No drama, no lies, no focus all on her. It's going to be a shock to go back to Texas in two days where the reality is swarmed by addiction. I don't think I'm ready.

Journal Entry 2

I know it sounds selfish, but I hope Amber going back inpatient doesn't mess up things for my brother and his wife coming to visit this weekend. Typically, when she gets admitted it clears things up and gives a bit of rest since we know she is completely safe for a few days. So maybe this is great timing. But then again, what if she escalates further? Will plans change so that I need to go to Texas? Man, Christmas packing would have been easier if I knew I'd be returning to Texas in only a few weeks, but that's probably a little too much deflection for one paragraph.

Journal Entry 3

I knew Amber had been drinking when she left for work today. Maybe it's pure selfish intent, but I don't want it on my conscience when she kills someone, whether it's herself or an innocent child. Should I call the cops to have them follow her after work to ensure my conscience is clear?

Update: I did it. I made the call. I told the cops her schedule, her home, and her information.

Journal Entry 4

I kind of get it, my mom is done with all of it so it's easier to avoid conflicts and not raise issues that are obviously not working. Just pretend like everything is fine. My dad, meanwhile, is so focused on helping her that he struggles to see outside of the immediate picture. Amber came in last night and threw a tantrum. My parents ran after her to appease her every need. Like why? I know, I know, they're afraid she's going to kill herself if they don't. But that's literally a tool in every addict and manipulator's toolbox. They know how much power it gives them because most humans don't want to cause someone else to end a life. The flaw is that addicts don't value their lives as much as they value their substances, so feelings and rationality cannot be considered equal parts of the typical equation. I don't know if that explains things or frustrates me more.

Journal Entry 5

I've realized I'm misplacing emotions toward Amber because if I took them out on everyone I was hurt by, I would have no one left. It's easier to focus on one person and be able to talk to my mom and dad and everyone else who, while impacted, still makes mistakes. Sure, I justify it with reasons like "wellllll my parents were stressed out by the most recent commotion or traumatized and therefore not acting like themselves." But the truth is, the one person who I blame is the one person who had the least ability to control herself.

3

Grief

SHORT STORY

Amber worked as an intern for Country Music Television. I had so much respect for her and thought she was such a badass to have such an incredible job. She was always interacting with celebrities and living this magic-filled life that she would tell me all about. Multiple times she got tickets for us to attend concerts for free. For one of these events, we spent a full day picking out outfits and putting makeup on while talking about every topic under the sun. Afterward, we walked around Nashville taking pictures at landmarks while re-singing our version of the recent concert. We were so carefree and just soaked in the nights, making memories, and deepening our relationship.

SUMMARY

It's weird to grieve someone who isn't dead. Grief is weird, I can technically get through the day. I can feel spits of joy, but then anything tedious like reading or studying will swirl around and dance up and down the pages of my mind. My brain can't zone in, and my heart can't calm down enough to rest or move on.

I used to be jealous of people whose addicts had passed away. I cringe writing it, but that part of me just wanted to grieve openly. I wanted people to understand my pain and see why I was so confused and broken. I wanted to be able to vocalize what I was going through. When you say you love an addict, no one knows what that really means. When you say you've lost a loved one, most people can at least somewhat relate. The truth is, I've lost a loved one, she just happens to physically be alive.

I've let myself mourn the loss of an aunt for my future children. I've mourned the maid of honor we always promised we would be at each other's weddings. I've mourned the memories and moments that I look back on now and see she was lying the entire time or pretending to be someone she thought I wanted her to be. Most of all though, I have mourned having a sister. That person you complain to about all of life's inconveniences. The person you call as you're getting ready for your dates and then right after to debrief each detail. The person you ask stupid questions to or send pictures of shoes to at eight in the morning to figure out which ones would be best for the day ahead. Sure, there are big things that I will never have because she chooses substances over me, but really, it's the little moments that tend to hit the hardest.

I started to wonder how I would describe addiction. Is there any way to put into words the horrors it brings? How do simple words portray the complexity and heartbreak to even a fraction of a degree? I've attempted these statements below to give at least a taste of the trials, but really, it's one of those things you hope no one ever has to truly live through or understand for themselves.

Letters to Addiction

- Addiction, (as the Little Rascals would say) I hate your stinkin' guts![1] But the problem is I don't always hate you. Because

1. McGowan, *Kid from Borneo*.

without you there are two alternatives. Obviously, we all hope for recovery, but what if it's the dreaded overdose? I'm grateful to still have my sister alive and addicted if it's compared to the latter option. What hurts most is not that she's addicted, but that everyone around me is drawn into this helpless circle as well. And that circle brings out many bad qualities and struggles of its own. If anyone thinks addiction is self-limited because it only affects the addict, they have obviously never helplessly watched their family go through it and fall apart. I think the worst part is I don't even know where to start. What am I supposed to do? I'm broken yet "untouched" so why is my pain so real? I'm not sure I even know who I am anymore. In a way, your addiction is driving me to an addiction of my own. One of worry and anxiety, sadness, and remorse. And unlike you, I won't deaden the pain that feels so real with a substance.

- Addiction is mourning the loss of someone while they physically still reside on earth. Just because hearts still beat and lungs still breathe does not mean the person you have known and loved still resides in the same body. I think we partially mourn the fact that our relationship is gone. Another part of us practices mourning since we know it's only a matter of time before the addiction takes our loved one from earth permanently.

- Addiction, oh addiction, you have taken more things than I can name. You've ruined more days than I can count and hurt more people than I know. You have stolen so many lives and broken so many homes. Why oh why are you so prevalent? Why is it that you can never totally be gone? It's like you have a million lives and every time one ends, you pop up yet again. I want to be mad, I'm filled with anger, but more than that, I'm filled with fatigue. I am so deeply exhausted and just want you to be gone. That day will never come, but maybe you could at least disappear from my life.

- The closest I can get to a definition is the idea of your best friend telling you the most heartbreaking, most hurtful thing you can think of and knowing there is absolutely nothing you can do to change their mind because they love a substance more than they are capable of loving you. Even in word form, it doesn't hold the weight and pain that comes with these actions, but I can't think of anything deeper.

JOURNALS

Journal Entry 1

It's nights like this that I wish she had just punched me or done some sort of physical harm so that I could at least visualize the pain being inflicted. Then, maybe I could heal from it, versus being trapped with her serenading lies continuously stabbing into me.

Journal Entry 2

My heart is heavy. The song "Worn" by Tenth Avenue North describes me tonight which, to be honest, adds insult to injury because my association with this band is my sister. I am struggling and that's okay. I feel like people always share their stories of conquering and overcoming. But that story at one time was in the middle of pain and chaos. If I can praise God at the end of this trial, surely I am capable of worshiping him in the dirt. Besides, haven't I always loved jumping in puddles and playing mud football? Maybe God was preparing me to have a messy life all along. This song is talking about wanting to simply know that the struggle ends. I think the hardest part about struggles is that there's no endpoint in sight. If we had a set requirement of days to make it through, or requirements to check off, then we could stare ahead at the beautiful end that's waiting. However, with real-life struggles, it's going day to day not knowing if you will be struggling forever, or if your victory sits moments away. Would I find it satisfying or discouraging to know my remaining days will be tumultuous? Would it be nice because I could plan for it, or would I become wary of the looming future? Realistically, my future will never be smooth. Once addiction entered my family, the future was forever altered. There's the hope of sobriety, but even with that comes the constant fear of relapse and the permanent damage that is too late to be repaired.

Journal Entry 3

I always thought knowing a missing person would be the deepest kind of pain to exist due to the lack of closure. At least with death, there's a definite answer. The pain might be worse, but at least you have an area to focus your grief on. With mystery, your mind floats in all different directions, and peace can never fully saturate it. I think addiction is the same way. Death brings on an entirely different set of pain, but it's one set battle. Hope is no longer a question, and the fluctuations are settled. Or there's the option of recovery, but even then, I imagine life would still revolve around the thoughts and fears of relapse. I think addiction is the equivalent of missing. The person is physically somewhere, but not present emotionally. You question daily if the person will be alive or dead, and the pain is constant.

Journal Entry 4

I feel as though my family is slowly dying in front of me. My sister definitely is.

Journal Entry 5

I think I've been distancing myself from everyone because I assume if I don't get attached then I can't get hurt. But that's not really living. I'm so conflicted. On the one hand, it does no good for me to know details of what goes on with my family because it just angers me, which doesn't positively impact anything. However, what if mom or dad had cancer right now? Me knowing wouldn't change anything prognosis-wise, yet I would still want to know. On the other hand, I'm acting like I don't have a sister, but the fact of the matter is, I do. It's entirely different to be born an only child and never experience a sibling. Once you have one, just plucking them out of your life doesn't remove their impact.

This also makes me realize I'm not ready for a boyfriend. I can't imagine telling someone all the brokenness and baggage that comes with me. There's a part of me who wants a man who understands the pain and can support me. There's something about misery that loves empathetic company. Then again, it would be nice to have some stability to balance out my dynamic family. Either way, it's going to take the deconstruction of my walls, and the ability to allow someone to truly know me. I talk about things I want in a significant other, but it is all going to start with a terrifying cascade of truth and revelation.

Journal Entry 6

I don't know how to love my sister. I think partially because I'm constantly preparing myself for the inevitable pain that's coming as she continues in her addiction. But in some ways, I think that might be an excuse.

Journal Entry 7

My heart is heavy thinking of all the losses addiction will bring me. It's taken away my sister, my future maid of honor, my children's aunt. My memories have become tinted, and my thoughts run in circles. No answer is simple, and no day is without worry. I need to come to terms with the very real possibility that I may never have my sister back. When was the last time, the last memory I have before addiction took her away? Even if she gets clean, will I ever truly trust her again? I think back to our pictures from our family trip to Hawaii when I had just graduated high school and she had just graduated college. I look at that summer as our last time really being together, but the reality is, she wasn't there. Even seven years ago, she was just at the level where she could hide it to keep her cover intact. What about my sophomore year in high school? That's when she stopped tennis and started having back issues. I have no memories of her at that time. Did she get hooked on painkillers? Did the medical community that I'm part of start this cascade? Does it change anything? Am I okay never actually knowing?

I need to be, because odds are, my answers will never come. I can't figure out why that bothers me. Why do I care that it's all a lie? Why do I care what caused what? Why do I care about any of it? It's all meaningless in the scheme of things . . . now if only my heart would believe that and stop hurting. I'm ready for my Revelation, when my tears will be wiped away and, more importantly, when my heart will beat again with a song, not the trudging drumbeat that keeps me alive, but really beats like the angels are playing a symphony in me and God's glory and hope will flow through my devastated body. One day my Revelation will come.

Journal Entry 8

It's Christmas time. I look outside and beautiful lights are adorning the surrounding trees and street lamps. I yearn to return to my youth. Back when I could sit there for hours and soak in the joy of flashing lights and look forward to the many mysteries of the season. Currently, all I can focus on is how scared I am about our family getting together. I'm traumatized from last year's yelling and tantrums. All I can think about are the future holidays that will be ruined by this horrible disease. I'm so confused, mad, frightened, and hurt. I wish I could just sit here and enjoy the flashing lights.

Journal Entry 9

I want to have a sister again, but I also know that enabling is the equivalent of killing an addict. I have been there to listen to my family's brokenness when time after time my sister crushes them. I was there, I remember going through those soul-wrenching moments years ago and it almost destroyed me.

Journal Entry 10

The alternative to not having a sister who is an addict would be to not have a sister at all. Amber as a person was bound to turn into an addict. It comes down to wondering if the pain is worth the memories. I would say it was. I can't imagine my childhood without her. I don't know who I would have played paper dolls with or pretended to be Sailor Moon with. That all would have been so lonely without her. So, with the two options I have, I choose life as I know it. It only hurts because our love runs so deep. That makes me cringe as I write it because it sounds so freaking cliché. It should practically be printed on canvas paintings for people to hang in their kitchens. Yuck! But I don't know how else to explain it. I love my sister, and the healthiest thing right now is to have a complete separation. I think one day I might be able to let her back into my life. Maybe just a tiny piece of her, but the future doesn't seem so despairing anymore. I have hope because my hope doesn't rely on her at all. My hope is in the fact that God will allow me to be okay, Amber is like a chocolate chip and I am brownies. Adding the chips to the brownies makes for a more enjoyable bite, but brownies are okay without them as well. I'm going to be okay.

Journal Entry 11

How messed up is it that sometimes I envy people who have lost their loved ones? I know that it would simply start an entirely new nightmare. I mourn the idea of not having any hope left. The idea of having that door completely shut is terrifying and overwhelming. I don't know if I could deal with that. Never mind, maybe I don't envy these people. I envy their ability to not live in limbo, but I mourn their actual lives and emotions.

Journal Entry 12

I hate it when people die. I've now had two friends be murdered by their loved ones' addictions. It makes my heart heavy and angry at an addiction that wasn't even their own. As much as I've made peace with Amber's addiction, there's still a part of me that hopes one day she will get help. I think hope is what makes so many trials possible. Without it, the world looks pretty dark.

Journal Entry 13

I want to look back on memories fondly. Right now, it doesn't matter which memory I try to recall, there's always something painful attached. For example, I hear any songs by Carrie Underwood and it brings me back to the concert where Amber left to "go to the bathroom" and missed out on what then was her favorite song. I was so worried she would miss the experience that I spent half the song looking for her and the other half recording it on my phone so that she could relive it. Later I learned she was getting drinks and just hadn't returned to our seats. Now anytime I see anything that is at all related to Carrie Underwood, I flash back to this memory. It's really frustrating because we have had a thousand good memories related to Carrie prior to this, yet that's the only one that fills my mind. I know this issue is in my mind, but I don't know how to fix it.

Journal Entry 14

It's not the big things you miss. Of course things like Christmas being destroyed by drunken shenanigans are not ideal. However, the big events have so many other factors that you can usually cope with distraction. It's the little things that sneak up on you. It's not wanting to throw away a specific beauty product because it might be the last thoughtful/sober-minded gift that came from her. It's hesitating to wear a certain shirt because of the memories you shared while wearing it. It's everyday life that really trips you up.

And then to top it all off, she's still alive. As hard as it is explaining everyday triggers, it's nothing compared to describing how you can mourn someone who is still alive.

They are still a part of every memory, emotion, and thought. I remember being four years old and going through a phase where I wouldn't let anyone wash my hair in the shower except Amber. Man, I would have been a dirty child if I didn't have her in my life. But in all seriousness, not knowing things often adds to the ongoing burden of heartbreak and anguish. The lack of understanding doesn't change the situation; it just increases the emotional strain. My tears still fall as I hear my mom whispering to my dad. Just because I don't know what specific devastation has happened doesn't change that life looks a little dimmer. Part of it is knowing how much my family is suffering and feeling selfish for not supporting them. But then again, I resent that they are all suffering yet refuse to try Al-Anon or set boundaries. It's a whole different kind of pain to step away. I think a huge part of my parents' anguish right now is that they were convinced quarantine had been great for my sister because she didn't have access to any substances and was forced to be clean the entire time. I've given up trying to explain the concept of alcoholism to them, yet a part of me keeps hoping they will suddenly wake up with a clarity that has to be self-found and desired. A piece of me is furious that they refuse to accept reality and as a result, they continually go through highs and lows. Why don't they trust me enough to believe what I tell them? If I wasn't physically living so far away, would they still be okay with me setting my boundary and severing contact?

4

Exhaustion

Amber has always been terrified of bridges. One weekend, Amber was driving me to a tennis tournament. As she drove us down this weird GPS-directed path, we came to an old rickety bridge that Amber refused to drive across. She didn't trust that it would support our car and didn't want to end up floating down the river. Her solution was to have me get out of the car and walk across it to prove that the bridge was stable and would hold the car. I'm still not completely sure what the logic of this was, but I remember fully trusting my sister and without hesitation jumping out of the car and walking across the bridge. I stopped directly in the middle and did a little dance. It was enough to convince her that it would be safe for the car, and she picked me up on the other side of the bridge. I miss being able to fully trust Amber without questioning the actual motivation behind her requests.

SUMMARY

There is no comparison to the exhaustion that addiction creates. It's like sprinting for ten miles, then moving a house, and saving a family from a fire kind of tired. Except you don't feel good or have endorphins from it. It hits suddenly. One moment you're hanging out, and the next you receive a text update from a family member, and you could fall to the ground and stay there for hours. I sometimes wonder if the body becomes so distracted that it forgets about the trauma building up in the mind. It's like every fiber of the body feels the growing pains and then immediately craves rest. Furthermore, when you can't express something, it slowly piles weight on your soul. It's impossible to explain being exhausted from the stress of the week and all the drama and unknowns that come with loving an alcoholic. *It's not just watching your sister slowly die in front of you, but seeing your parents as mere skeletons of who they used to be*, from the toll addiction has taken on them. It takes time, emotions, and physical energy, really everything becomes impacted to the core. To top it off, there's no true rest because nightmares are looming anytime you close your eyes. For those few times you dare to attempt rest, there's a piece of you that is always alert to the triggering sounds of ringtones and text messages that might signal the world crashing down. Your body has been trained to assume the worst. So even with rest, there's a part of the brain always alert for the terrifying ringtone of death. It all combines to create complete and utter exhaustion.

JOURNALS

Journal Entry 1

I've been watching some television in my free time and, at first, I thought it was dramatic how every episode has a catastrophe in it. Then it hit me, my family could have been a reality show, and it wouldn't need to be scripted. There are plenty of tragedies, dramatic events, and nerve-wracking moments to fill countless hours of nighttime entertainment. I focus on the fact that I've had a somewhat crazy life, but it makes me wonder if this is the norm. Maybe life is just a crazy ride. Instead of a slick, paved road that goes fast, it's a twisty, bumpy, dirt road that flings dust up to remind you of the past as you go.

Journal Entry 2

Mom called and said I sounded tired. I wish people would realize "tired" is my cover. I'm only tired because I'm drained from life. Anytime I say I'm tired, I actually mean I'm going through a lot and don't want to talk about it. This sounds the opposite of wanting someone to realize I'm struggling, but it's the principle of someone realizing that I'm having a hard time and being there to support me. I want a hug, even better, a big-dog hug with lots of licks and tail wagging to remind me that someone is excited to have me in their life and support me.

Journal Entry 3

I feel exhausted all the time. It might be from the constant emotional stress, but how does one learn how to have happy and calm dreams? I'm sure there are other things, too, but eight hours of high-intensity dreams seems like it would exhaust anyone.

Journal Entry 4

My nightmares have been back for weeks now. I forget what it's like to get a normal night of sleep and not be terrorized for hours at a time. I think my dreams are how I can judge how I'm doing. I can smile or cry each day, but those can be manipulated to wait until I'm alone or get through the day at school. However, each night I close my eyes and hope for sweet peace, and I have no control over what the next hours hold.

Journal Entry 5

I haven't heard from my mom today which makes me assume there must be a mess going on in Texas. I'm so over it and so utterly depressed along with ferociously angry. I need to punch something but I'm too exhausted to fathom working up the strength for that.

Journal Entry 6

I'm exhausted by it all. This is supposed to be a restful Christmas break from classes, but in reality, I can't wait to get back to school. Life is so much clearer from a distance. I so appreciate being away in Colorado and having a few states between me and the chaos. Constantly waiting for the next blow-up or tragedy is more than I can take, I just want to sleep for days and let my body finally get the rest it needs.

Journal Entry 7

I've been on a bit of a depressive sabbatical. I couldn't function and was so overwhelmed, but I'm doing better now. I'm ready to start fresh and get better. I haven't heard anything about Amber in over two weeks, and I think that's helping too.

Journal Entry 8

I wish every aspect of addiction didn't take out every bit of strength I have. I had a brief conversation and let two friends in on the smallest of details about living with addiction. I didn't even go into how it impacted me, yet it still put a haze over the rest of the day. My mind is pulsing, and my eyes are watering. I guess it didn't help that I texted Mom and she just wanted to complain about Amber. Why can't she just respond to my funny cat picture with a laughing face? How horrible does it sound that I want my mom to lie about her emotions so that it can be easier on me? I'm just struggling so much.

Journal Entry 9

My soul longs for peace. The kind of peace that only comes from Christ. I've lived my life proclaiming it, so why am I struggling so much to simply grasp it? I'm tired down to my joints, but not by any means physically. It's a constant emotional battle waging inside my mind. I know I need to talk about it, I can feel the emotions and instability rising by the day, but I continue holding onto my tiny piece of false control in order to function. I know it will all spill out at the most inconvenient time this way. I am in survival mode. It's a goal of functioning, not necessarily thriving. A part of me hates that, but also functioning is me giving 100 percent and working at my full capacity so I guess that's something.

5

Mixed Signals/Confliction

SHORT STORY

Something my siblings and I have in common is our unfortunate dental alignment. Because of this, we all spent time with braces and headgear. I remember so many nights where we would sulk and hide, trying to avoid our adjustments. Our poor parents were stuck with putting these contraptions on our heads each night. As adults, we are all incredibly grateful to have straight teeth, but at the time we couldn't understand how something that caused pain could be a good thing, it was very confusing. Most trials in life tend to produce similar emotions. In the moment, the pain feels overwhelming— but with time, you begin to see the beauty that emerged from it. Looking back, you not only appreciate the outcome, but also the unexpected joys along the way, like indulging in extra ice cream and pudding after each adjustment.

SUMMARY

Everything in life has multiple sides. Part of what makes addiction so challenging is the combination of emotions that make you feel like you're on a roller coaster and there's no definitive up or down, just lots of flipping around. There's the internal division of wanting to have emotional layers of protection, while simultaneously knowing time with addicts tends to be limited. We have a deep desire to absorb all moments, good or bad. There's also a constant yearning to share life with the person who used to be such a daily staple. That person who you want advice and approval from, yet know you can't break your boundary to trust. To further complicate it, temporary sobriety isn't always a happy ending for an addict. The deepest desire is always sobriety. However, the fear of how many people overdose after leaving rehab sits high on the back burner. There is always going to be the dream of a sober future, but that doesn't diminish the fears and repercussions that rehab brings.

Moreover, there's a conflict of feeling forgotten yet remaining too afraid to tell people what's really going on or to need attention. You're wanting people to realize what's going on yet the desire to hide the truth from everyone overrides that craving. You want to be in charge of anything at all because everything feels overwhelming, yet you can't take control because you end up hiding from everything.

JOURNALS

Journal Entry 1

Something challenging is going to visit my family on breaks or vacations. When I return to school people always ask how it was. The truth is, it is fun to see my family and it is good to see the house I grew up in. However, there's always going to be screaming battles, there may be an ER trip. And many times, I'll lock myself in my room to sleep because no one knows if my sister will do anything harmful or not. So yes, there are good parts to visiting family, but there are also parts that, after returning from "vacation," I haven't been able to wrap my mind around. There are parts that scare me and parts that mess with my focus for weeks to come, but explaining that to everyone who asks me seems a bit outrageous. Instead,

I tend to find some answer that isn't technically a lie but doesn't come close to covering the entire truth. It's enough to get me by, but every time I tell it, a part of me questions if I'm bending my morals to cover up the fact that my family is a mess.

Journal Entry 2

I realized today that Amber is so far removed from my life because it has truly been years since I had any closeness with her. Simultaneously, I'm realizing that because I've watched this slow progression of addiction dissolving her life, I haven't noticed all the gradual changes. It's astonishing how utterly different she is. There were little changes constantly happening, so I didn't realize she had so drastically transformed. I sit here tonight wondering if I want her back in my life. I can't imagine a reality where I could ever trust her again or have any type of relationship that wouldn't break me down. Yet I also struggle to imagine my life without her forever.

This all started with me trying to find a picture of Amber to show my roommate why I couldn't recognize my sister anymore. I went back two years to my brother's wedding to find the picture I ended up using, but realistically I know she was already struggling with alcohol at that point. I wanted an earlier picture which is when I realized it would be when we were in Nashville together and she was wasted in many of those pictures as well.

I truly wonder what Amber's story is. I'm reading the *Big Book* and going through stories of different alcoholics.[1] I wonder if I will ever truly know her story and what events either escalated or eventually saved her.

Journal Entry 3

I never realized punching a mirror could cause so much satisfaction. I accidentally broke my mirror earlier and realized how easily it snapped. It made me want to take control of something,

1. Wilson, *Alcoholics Anonymous.*

and somehow, that turned into me destroying my mirror with my knuckles. I know things are beyond terrible in Texas, and I know that potentially graduating late because of COVID won't be affected by anything I do. I know that my depression is flaring up even though I'm taking my meds, and I know that there's a possibility that COVID will flare up again, and everything will get even more insane than it currently is. There's just so much out of my control that I want to be in charge of something. Maybe punching a mirror is a stupid thing to be in charge of, but it's something. And who knows, maybe it puts me in a group of some sort. Right now, I feel separated from my family because I decided to stay distanced from addiction updates. I feel separated from my friends because it's not fair to put the burden entirely on them and I don't want to monopolize our time together with my problems. But I'm all mixed up and I don't even know how I feel. It's like each color of Play-Doh is a different emotion and they are all mashed together into a weird conglomeration. That crazy combination of colors is me. And I think that's okay, but I don't know what to do with it. The only person I feel like I can really talk to about this stuff is my therapist. What does it say about me that I have to pay someone to listen to my problems? What does it say about me that I'm constantly in a state of chaos? Do other people have stable lives, or do they simply compartmentalize, hide, or just cope better in general?

Journal Entry 4

The other day at church, one of my pastors asked me how I was doing. I did my classic beat around the bush and said, "Living the dream." He then asked me three more times, I gave some false poetic answers that 99 percent of the time results in people smiling and continuing their days. But not him, he called me out. He said, "Yes, but how are you actually doing?" I wish I could just be honest and say when I'm having a hard time, but I have this block when it comes to trusting anyone with my emotions. I know it stems back to not wanting people to know me for fear of what they might find out, but it makes me want it even more. It's like my greatest fear is what I most desire. There's probably something deep about that but my brain isn't astute enough to connect what it is.

Journal Entry 5

A friend was talking today about how she wished she had embraced the few years her addicted sibling was sober because now that her sibling is dead, she would give anything to embrace those years. I'm so torn. On one hand, I want to call Amber right now and soak in every moment I have. Addicts live on a different timeline. I likely only have years instead of decades, but I don't know. I have to remember that my boundary is not simply a choice; instead, it is deeply rooted in heartbreaking pain. There would be so many wounds reopened if I established a relationship. I think part of having a boundary is so I don't have to use my mental energy to constantly wonder if I should break it down. There are so many reasons that my boundary is necessary, but it's so easy to forget when I'm seeing the drama from a distance.

Journal Entry 6

Today was a picture-perfect day. My friends and I visited the Great Sand Dunes and played like kids, rolling down hills, making sand castles, and just enjoying the ambiance. Running down the dunes was a mix of adrenaline, laughter, and comfort. Afterward, we went to a hidden waterfall and it was breathtaking, powerful and gentle at the same time. At one point on our drive, we stopped at a beautiful field covered in yellow flowers, it was like a fairy tale.

I want to focus on the good. There's so much incredible stuff happening! But how do I authentically block out all the hurt and pain happening back home? I feel guilty knowing that the rest of my family is stressed and struggling right now while I'm out enjoying myself.

Journal Entry 7

My brother started a group message where we all picked our favorite Thanksgiving foods and Amber picked sushi, so I picked pizza based on a picnic the two of us had one year. Then she said, "Love you boo boo." It felt so good to have an olive branch and even one day of having my sister back. But I also hate that I have to be on guard constantly. I have to remind myself that it's not her making this an issue, it's me putting a boundary because it's what's healthiest for me and the only way to survive this mess of a life. I want to soak in the warmth of having a sister for today, but there are so many other feelings that cloud the smile. I worry about what she's trying to manipulate by reaching out. I worry my courage and strength to keep up boundaries will falter, I worry my emotions won't be able to handle the whiplash of this, but I also want to have at least a few hours of feeling normal. And when I think about the truth it ruins those few good moments, so I think for at least the next thirty minutes I'll let myself stay in sweet oblivion.

Journal Entry 8

I know I'm not handling things the best way, but I don't know how to do any better, so I guess in a way I am doing the best because it's the best that I'm able to do. I know Amber is manipulating . . . she is in the beg-for-attention/suck-up mode that means tomorrow or the next day she will be in the guilt-trip/terror/tantrum mode. In some ways, it's comforting to have a rhythm because otherwise, it's just living on edge waiting for the next tantrum. At least this way I'm living, knowing it's about to come, and not falling into the illusions or manipulations between them. The only problem with this is that it forces me to miss all the good moments that happen between the drinking and terrors. I only experience the bad because I block out the good . . . but it's so easy for me to let my guard down, and I know as soon as I do, she never fails to jump in and do her best to destroy my heart with all that she has. I'm tired. Maybe I can avoid her and avoid that situation altogether.

Journal Entry 9

Amber is on something. I could tell when she came in and made comments about how important she was to my dad's dog. Later at dinner, her cat came up to the table and tried to paw up to the table where sushi was. I yelled at him so he wouldn't eat my sushi. Amber threw a fit about how I hadn't talked to her in two weeks yet how dare I yell at her cat. It doesn't matter that I take care of this pet every night that I'm here since she's always passed out drunk; that, of course, gets forgotten. I hate that for the rest of the night I'm on eggshells because I just don't want to deal with it. I know at some point she's going to bring up wanting to talk and I'm nervous about it because I know it will just be her in a drunk state trying to make me feel bad so she can have some power, but I hate that I have to deal with it. I'm sitting here in a state of nerves trying to avoid it. I'm just really tired.

Let time take time.

Journal Entry 10

I just left my parents' house. I can feel the churning of sweet relief combined with exhaustion. For the first time since being in Texas, I'm not sleeping with caution waiting for a scream from my parents that signifies my sister overdosed. I'm not hiding behind screens to avoid difficult conversations with my sister that she won't remember, but will be seared into my heart. I'm not second-guessing every sound and smell as that of alcohol, drugs, or sneaky behavior. I'm simply existing. My shoulders have already lowered at least two inches from that lack of stress. I'm also incredibly tired as I'm finally letting my body relax after weeks of the high-stress tension that ruled it 24/7. I'm proud to have such a healthy body that withstood the trial, but it's time for some recuperation before classes start back up.

I'm reading *Through the Eyes of a Lion*. The section I'm on now is talking about how pain is a microphone that opens conversations and opportunities that would otherwise have been out of reach.[2] It talks about not being selfish with your pain and sharing it with others. I think that may give me motivation when reflecting on this trial. At least I hope it does. How great would it be to look back in a year and realize lives were changed because of this one trial? God is good. And as far as addiction reaches, I know he will have someone I can share with who is also struggling with these same fears, heartaches, and daily life.

Good night journal, time to sleep and see what new adventures tomorrow is to bring.

Journal Entry 11

Mom said she worries about me. On the one hand, I feel validated that she's thinking about me. But I don't want to add to the mess of things that she's already dealing with, so I feel like I need to filter what I share.

Journal Entry 12

I was the first person in my family to admit my sister had a problem and distance myself from her. This was after talking with a counselor, going to AA meetings as I attempted to understand her, and regularly attending Al-Anon. It took me a while to get past the anger, hurt, and pain to finally come to a point where I could legitimately, with no anger, set a boundary. I was able to take a step back and know that it truly was best for both Amber and me. I finally realized that this was the only way she would be forced to stop manipulating me and have to face life. With this, I got a lot of backlash. It broke my heart that my family would believe the lies my sister was telling instead of asking me for the whole story. They knew enough at that point to understand she was an alcoholic, but they brushed it off as a temporary thing that she would overcome with enough love and support. Since she was the sick one, she was the one who gathered support. It didn't seem to matter that my

2. Lusko, *Through the Eyes of a Lion*, 108.

heart was shattered too. All that anyone could see was her sickness. The problem is, it hurt me even more when my family finally understood because the same pains were placed on them. When my brother called me with brokenness in his voice, I would have done anything for him to not experience the pain that forced me to set a boundary. I still wait for the day some of my loved ones realize why I have set my line and how hard it is for me to keep it. But until then, I know she will be seen as the victim, and I will be seen as the antagonist.

Journal Entry 13

I wonder what it says about me that I constantly assume people are being manipulative or passive-aggressive in my family. I've been hurt too many times to be willing to change that thinking, but it is an intriguing phenomenon that the motivations could be pure at times.

6

Terror

SHORT STORY

When I was around six years old, I got stuck in an elevator at church. It was my fault and not an electrical problem. I was hitting the wrong button and then couldn't figure out why nothing was happening. I remember when the door finally opened, my face was blotched from crying, and I made an instant resolution to always take the stairs. My tiny mind had convinced me that I was either going to crash and die in this elevator or be stuck there and forced to live in a five-by-five-foot square for the rest of my life. My sister immediately went to the craft room and made me a "safety doll" out of a wooden rod, some material, and a can lid. She told me the doll would be with me anytime I got scared or felt alone. This is the kind, loving sister I grew up with. Someone who would jump into action the moment someone was having a hard time or struggling. This is her true character, beneath the addiction.

SUMMARY

How do you sum up the anxieties and fears that constantly copilot your days? From being terrified of phone calls and doorbells because of what they represent, to fearing for your safety. There are little triggers everywhere that flare up memories, no matter how hard you try to be neutral. It's impossible to walk into a room and not notice at least one thing that drops your stomach. The worst tends to be phones, which is quite inconvenient since everyone has their phones around constantly. Any chirp of a text message or singing or a ringtone fills my heart with dread since bad news is communicated this way. It doesn't matter what time of day it is, the first thought with any ringtone is that devastation has once again entered my life. There's the fear *for* your loved one and the life they are losing. Always waiting for the text or call that says she is never waking up again. Always tiptoeing around conversations because it's a very real possibility it will be your last conversation with her. However, there's also the fear *of* your loved one and the pain they are causing. Constantly worrying about the potential car wrecks from their inebriation. Continually being afraid of the words they will say, and how those will impact your thoughts. Cascading fears about other family members with their health and mental status as they, too, are living in constant chaos. Never having a break since nighttime brings a whole new set of fears with the constant nightmares.

JOURNALS

Journal Entry 1

It's the little things that trigger me. Tonight, a package was delivered from Amazon and, following the doorbell, my parents went to retrieve it. I stayed in the other room, and until they both came back happy, I was convinced it was someone coming to tell us Amber had overdosed or caused a car crash. I can't stop my mind from assuming the worst and being terrified until I hear her come safely through the front door.

Journal Entry 2

Dad will do everything in his power to save Amber, and that's my biggest fear. I truly believe the idea of not being able to help her may kill him. He may be incapable of accepting the reality of a daughter he can't help. It's not his fault, we were all raised the same, but to him, I think he sees it as his responsibility to provide a life where she can thrive.

Journal Entry 3

I got back from town and Amber was leaving with our dog in her car. I was furious. The entire time she was away I was racked with terrors of never seeing that sweet pooch alive again due to her crashing in her altered state. I came up to my room and read Al-Anon literature and the Bible to calm down, but it wasn't until I heard that sweet doggo's paws patter through the door that I could actually breathe. My stomach is still in knots and I'm furious that she put me through this. I know it was my own choice to react that way, but it's one thing if she risks her own life, it's another to risk the life of our dog. My head is a really weird place to be these days.

Journal Entry 4

I had a nightmare last night that Amber and Mom were fighting and then Amber came up to my room. I can't remember if she was going to physically hurt me or mentally abuse me. Either way, I can still feel the anxiety of holding my breath by the door frame, trying to be still so she would run by me and then be able to spring out and have a head start on her. The problem was I was too scared to move, so I stood stranded by the door, completely at her mercy to do or say whatever she wanted. It did make me realize why I'm so

SIBLING OF AN ALCOHOLIC

terrified of her, which I guess is a good thing. Our society looks at physical abuse as terror, and it hasn't made sense to me why I'm so incredibly terrified of Amber until now. Growing up, I didn't fear pain, probably because I never had a reason to. The only times I got hurt were from playing sports or trying stunts like jumping off of random objects, etc., things that I deserved to be hurt by because I shouldn't have been attempting them in the first place. However, verbal abuse was quite different. I remember being too scared to confront the lies that bullies told me because that tiny ounce of possibility that someone else could confirm the lies or think the same horrible things would have been too much for me to handle. Instead, I held on to all the lies and harbored them as insecurities for years. College was an amazing time for me where I truly learned who I was and how to be me and not this version of myself who was just trying to survive from one day to the next. I forgot what it was like to live in fear of invalidation and dejection, where you've stepped onto the point of nothingness.

It's weird that, even though I know Amber only says things to me when she's drunk, they still impact me as if she were sober. Even as I sit here typing, I get a feverish sensation at the possibility she could send me a message or do something else to hurt me that I have no control over. I guess naming it and figuring it out is kind of important in the scheme of working on flaws, so maybe this is a good start.

Journal Entry 5

I have officially moved to Colorado and completed my first week of school. Turmoil doesn't begin to cover it. What if I can't do this? What if I can't handle the added stress to my already crazy life? I want to be enough. I want to be a sparkle of hope, so my parents don't need to worry about me. However, the idea of failure cripples me. My family is falling apart, and it puts a dark tint on everything around me. I don't feel like I belong. Everyone is so optimistic, happy, outdoorsy, and honestly very similar to the me I previously was. I feel void, empty, sad. This is a fresh start and I want to have a clean slate, but fear holds tight.

I carry a stun gun and knife with me at all times because the area I live in is super sketchy. Constant crimes are being committed to the point of the police telling us it isn't a safe place for people my age to be. My friends joke about how paranoid I am, and I laugh with them because it's easier to laugh than to explain the terrifying reality that's forced me to learn how unsafe this world is. I miss the trusting, naive version of myself who freely loved and didn't worry. I wonder if it's better to live in reality or to revert and blindly walk into danger.

I'm frightened and exhausted. I just want to blissfully sleep without the nightmares and without the sinking feeling that I'm going to get a call saying my life has forever changed because my sister won't be waking up.

Journal Entry 6

Today has been hard. This past week has been hard. I'm struggling. As my sponsor says, I'm grieving. I miss having a sister. Today in school, we're learning about suicide and toxic ingestion. Both things Amber tends to do frequently—well, attempt at least. I guess you can't succeed at suicide multiple times. I'm realizing that I'm angry, furious actually. Not because I'm mad at anything but because I'm terrified. I'm so scared of what the future holds. I'm terrified that if one family member kills themselves, statistically other family members also have a higher incidence rate. I'm terrified that I won't be able to focus on this class or get through all of it because of how distracted I am, and how much I'm struggling. I'm so mad about the little things. I'm realizing that it's because I'm so scared and so sad. This all took me about an hour of intense exercise to finally calm my mind to a place of understanding.

I talked with my psychiatrist today. He probes different areas of my thinking. He helps me explore my thought processes and decipher my feelings. I'm so glad I ended up in his office for help.

Journal Entry 7

My heart is so heavy tonight. My grief is almost overwhelming. I want a sister. Even more than the grief of that is all the thoughts and emotions flooding back from Amber's suicide attempts. I thought I had processed these things and moved forward. I feel so immersed in those memories that I can hardly breathe. I'm scared. I'm hurt. I'm sad. My sponsor tells me to lean into the emotions so that I can feel and process them. But I hate feeling things, it's painful. However, I do think part of the reason it's so agonizing now is because I've dodged and weaved for so long.

I talked with Mom yesterday and she has come to the same conclusion. Amber has her own higher power in God. It is her relationship and no matter what we do, we can't change her or help her if she doesn't want it. This is the healthiest I've heard mom sound; I don't know where dad falls in this thinking, but I was really impressed at her thoughts. My mind immediately jumps to the fear that Dad will be on a totally opposite page. If anything happens to Amber, Dad will blame Mom and she will blame him with the potential result of their marriage falling apart. I know that's worst-case-scenario thinking, but things in our family tend to fall on the worst-case spectrum.

I'm proud of myself for doing self-care this afternoon. I couldn't handle the content of class with the topics of addiction and suicide. Instead, I skipped out two and a half hours early and went on a run followed by sprints until I finally wore my body out to a point where I could process things. I've never skipped class in my life, which makes me all the more proud that I listened to my body. For once, I did what was best for me and didn't follow rules simply because they were there.

Journal Entry 8

Mom went to someone's play or something tonight, which isn't important except for the fact that she left the house to get away. If she's leaving, then that means Amber is driving again. It also means that she is scheduling things to purposefully be away from my dad, which terrifies me.

Journal Entry 9

My cup is waterfalling over, there are no dribbles. It's glaciers dropping in and gushing huge volumes all over, creating a gigantic mess. I can't add anything else to the mix. I don't know if I can even handle the mix as it currently is. I hate that I'm so impacted. I want to be okay. But I'm realizing that I'm not. Addiction is back in my life. Technically it never left, but it has now lurked out of its shadows and I'm having to deal with all the pain that goes with it.

Journal Entry 10

I was talking with my brother the other day. He started writing a letter to our parents talking about how worried he was about Amber, and his concerns about dad giving her money, believing her lies, etc. It was really well written, and I was impressed at his expression of delicate matters. However, in the end, he decided not to send it. He was worried about the very real possibility that Amber could overdose in the next week or two after the letter was received, but without time to react or change things. He doesn't want our parents to feel increased guilt or add to their pain.

I can laugh off how messed up things are, most of the time, and talk about deep, horrifying things as if I'm describing a new CD collection. In a similar way to how kindergartners come home and talk about their day, I talk about mine. This is typically without much emotion, simply reciting facts, nothing more or less . . . until times like these. Of course I know that my sister is killing herself. Of course I know she's an alcoholic. I'm the one who has been begging and pleading for people to listen to me and get help for her. Yet there's still that piece of me that begs with myself, pleading that I'm wrong. Hoping fiercely that I've blown things out of proportion, and I'm an overdramatic millennial who craves attention. And then things like this happen, and I can't trick that part of me like I normally can. I can't make up some excuse or validation that explains or comforts the reason my brother can't send his letter. The truth is, he's absolutely correct. At this exact moment, she's more likely to die from addiction than live with it. I don't know why that breaks my heart so much more tonight, but it's like I'm caught in a nightmare again, only this time I know it will be forever if she continues. Alcohol or drugs will kill her, and our lives will turn into a nightmare that can't be awoken from. I guess one could argue that our lives are already an unawakenable nightmare, but at least with this terror there's hope that sparkles behind the clouds. There are stars in the sky that remind us light exists. When she ends this, the stars will no longer shine for her, and that's devastating to the core.

Journal Entry 11

At times it feels hard to breathe and my mind is spinning in dizzy circles. I feel overwhelmed but I don't know what I'm overwhelmed about. Part of me wants to try and run five miles to calm down, part of me wants to sit in the shower and cry, and part of me is too confused to know what's going on. Most recently, I sat down to study and my chest felt like it was on fire, not like heartburn. It was the physical skin, my entire outside, but only my chest was burning up. I went to get ice cream because, clearly, that would solve everything. I figured it would cool me down, but I felt so off-balanced and jittery the whole time. It was hard to get the spoon from the bucket to my mouth. I was convinced I would drop it from shaking. I sat there and ate Nutella and ice cream and focused on breathing. My pulse wasn't racing and nothing else happened, so maybe this was just a glitch in my system or something like a pre-panic attack. Golly gee, I did not enjoy it, it was scary not having control over my body. Probably a sign I should start relaxing more.

Journal Entry 12

Four high school students were killed by a drunk driver last night. There's so much heartbreak and pain even though I didn't personally know any of them. I feel for my community. It also fills me with terror at the idea of how easily Amber could have been the cause of it. Just because she hasn't hit any people yet doesn't mean she won't. She's gotten in multiple small wrecks that we know of, which means time is running out before there is another vehicle involved. I'm terrified of living with that potential reality. I know my therapist would say, "That's thinking in an all-or-nothing mindset." With her history, I don't think it's that farfetched to lean toward that being a likely reality. It adds an additional reason why I'm angry with her. If her friends and family aren't enough of a reason for her to get help, then why aren't these kids? How ironic is it that she wants to be a school counselor, yet she is potentially the reason many kids are going to require counseling?

Journal Entry 13

I woke up from a nightmare where I was being brutally tortured, yet I felt cool as a cucumber. Honestly, I much prefer the physical to emotional nightmares.

Journal Entry 14

I'm sitting in my bed working, and all I can think about with every noise is, "I hope Amber doesn't try to come into my room." I don't think she would be violent, but I know she would say horrible things, and I don't want to put those in my mind right now. I can never quite relax until I turn the lights out and can pretend I'm asleep if nothing else.

Journal Entry 15

I hate sitting around waiting to be the bad guy. How is it that she can turn my birthday into a terrifying day I'm dreading? I know she wants to have a heart-to-heart because she's inebriated and I'm going to have to be the bad guy and say, No, I'm not moving my boundary. Logic means nothing because once again, she's completely under the influence. Unfortunately, that doesn't stop the curdling feeling in my stomach from forming, or my breath from catching in my throat. I debate if vomiting would help or just add to my helpless feelings. The jury is out, but I think I hope to avoid it for now.

I watched Amber's face for a bit and her emotions were real. Do the substances actually numb her, or in some ways do they amplify her emotions? I wonder if I could handle seeing what is going on inside her mind.

7

Forgotten

SHORT STORY

When I was in college, our tennis team went to Florida for spring break and played various matches throughout the state. Amber was living in Florida at the time and met up with me one of the nights. She took me to get the biggest milkshake I'd ever seen. We talked, laughed, and caught up on life. We had that friendship on top of our sisterhood where we could go weeks without talking and then as soon as we saw each other, it was like we were back in elementary school sharing a room and sharing our lives. The fact that she went out of her way and wanted to spend time and know me was priceless. At that time, I deeply admired her and couldn't imagine why she would spend time with me when I was nowhere as cool as she was. Sometimes it's the littlest activities that create the biggest memories.

SUMMARY

Most of the time I'm outwardly okay. I can be present and support my parents. Even more, I'm able to live my life in a way that people don't see what's going on behind my smile. Most days I can balance the weight of emotional baggage that used to drive me to outbursts of big, ugly tears. I have largely mastered the act of compartmentalizing things so much that I can separate family, school, and social events. While there's no way to completely keep things separate, this strategy has kept me able to focus, able to survive. However, there are days when, despite all the coping techniques and therapy, I'm still not okay. Days when all my weights try to drag me down and it's too much work to stand up, much less talk to people or go about my day as normal. Those are the days when being a sibling of an alcoholic is devastating. Growing up, you go to your parents if things are hard. However, now my life revolves around my sister's addiction. If my bad day aligns with one of her episodes, then she has to be the priority. And looking at it from the outside, it should be that way. After all, she's the one who's sick and she's the one who needs help immediately. However, you can only be put on the back burner for so long before you start questioning your validity and worth. You can only have so many days where you have no one to go to before you start to give up. Friends are great, and Al-Anon is amazing, but deep down you want to talk to someone who really gets it. Someone who is in the same situation as you, but that's the catch. *Everyone in your position is too distracted to help you, and everyone who can help you doesn't fully understand what it's like.*

JOURNALS

Journal Entry 1

If addiction was any other illness, there would be a completely different reaction. For example, if my sister had a chronic autoimmune disease and ended up hospitalized, I would talk about it and hear people praying for her. It would be acceptable for me to take a day or two to process things, and I wouldn't have to explain why my emotions are all over the place. As it is, the secret remains. Bitter emotions fill my family, lies begin to form, and disagreements happen. No one agrees on how to treat her or how to hold her accountable. I am grateful that while she is an inpatient, her car is out of her possession, just temporarily, but it's a win I'll settle for. I need to study so I can pass my exam on Friday. However, my mind spins or, more accurately, swirls like a paintbrush controlled by a toddler who dabbles in little bits of all the colors and winds up with a bland, brown result. Once again I find myself wanting to be comforted, wanting to not be so isolated by this horrible disease.

Journal Entry 2

I'm twenty-six today, mom called to say Happy Birthday and ended up talking about stupid stuff Amber has been doing. It hurts that today is my day and it still ends up focused on Amber. Why can't I get used to this and get over it? I don't want it to impact me, but I'm feeling it tonight. I'm sad. I had an incredible day, everyone loved me so well, and yet I'm sad.

Journal Entry 3

I'm furious. Past furious, I hate that my sibling always gets the attention. I'm not okay, but I feel like I can't tell my family that because they are already dealing with so much. I'm constantly worrying about the toll addiction is taking on everyone, and I'm terrified of making things any more complex or painful than they already are. What if I'm the straw that breaks my parents' backs?

Journal Entry 4

Dad texted to update me and ask how I was doing. I never tell the truth when he asks, but I decided to tell a sliver of the truth, and say I was okay. Saying that I'm having a super rough night, totally overwhelmed, and exhausted seemed like it might freak him out. Instead, I stuck with okay and explained some of the things I'm struggling with. He never responded. That really hurts. A piece of me was vulnerable and he didn't even respond. Of course, then

I jump to over-analyzing: maybe he thinks I was being passive-aggressive, maybe something happened to Amber and he's protecting me until after my exam tomorrow, or, worse, maybe he read it and had a heart attack or stroke. This is exactly what it's like to have Amber out of the hospital, a million worries and a million exclusions from my parents. It's never on purpose but always just as painful.

Journal Entry 5

I feel distracted. My heart is breaking, my mind is tumbling, and I don't know who to talk to. It feels like my world is crashing down and I feel isolated in my gut-wrenching agony.

Girls at work were comparing stories of how their dads had checked in on them and missed them. I know I'm missed and my life is simply overshadowed by the mess of my sister. But that distraction is one of the many reminders of how messy our normal life is, and how much it hurts.

I took this summer job so that I could avoid going to Texas. Am I being selfish? Do my parents need me more than work does? Am I strong enough to help at home?

The lyrics from Tenth Avenue North's song "Worn" are comforting my soul tonight. I'm trying to come to a place where I can accept and know things fall into place without Amber being healed.

Journal Entry 6

I just talked with my mom and she said, "You know I love you, right?" I have so many mixed feelings. My mind is a hot mess, so of course the first thing I do is catastrophize. I assume that she's considering suicide and must be calling to say bye to me.

I can't imagine how hard Mom has it with everything going on. I really don't think it's selfish to focus on myself, it's what's important for my healing right now. However, that doesn't mean my parents aren't struggling worse than me. On a more upbeat note, it really did remind me that my parents care about me too. I've always known they love me, but it does take its toll to always be second string. I understand sickness and the required attention, but the healthy struggle too. I think it's honestly the fact of how taboo alcoholism is. I could list the many validations I have, but I need to admit it's a balance. There's a place for my boundaries and it's okay to set limits that are healthy for me. However, there is also going to be a time when grace and love need to penetrate that wall. I don't know if it's justified, but I think it's okay that I'm not to that point yet. I'm still building my boundary; actually, I think it's built. But it takes time to find out where I can chisel a hole to drain my watery feelings while not affecting the infrastructure.

Journal Entry 7

I called Dad yesterday and he texted back today mentioning very general things that were going well and then immediately jumped into the improvements Amber has been making. I don't want to talk about Amber. I want my dad to stop centering his life around her and see that I miss him. In the movie *My Sister's Keeper* Anna says, "I'm important too, I'm important too."[1] I can't help but feel this is relatable. Just because I seem okay doesn't mean I don't need my parents. And I know it's not fair to blame them when I make it a full-time job to pretend I'm fine, but it still hurts.

Journal Entry 8

Mom just texted and told me that our cat was not going to make it through the night. Her next sentence was, do you think I should tell Amber or not? In the course of six days, it's been confirmed my grandma has breast cancer, my sister has told me I am to blame for her trying to kill herself, and now our sweet cat of fifteen years is dying.

1. Cassavetes, *My Sister's Keeper*.

God, I know you're pushing me until I depend on you, well you win! I can't even fake a smile. I can't pretend anymore. I'm past broken, I'm disintegrated. Lord, please help me survive this.

Journal Entry 9

Our sweet cat died. This week has been trial after trial after trial. It is going to take every last ounce of me to get through my final exam tomorrow. Mom texted me that Dad told Amber about the cat. First of all, I'm hurt that Mom hasn't checked to see how I'm doing. I loved that cat as much as Amber and took care of her for many more years. It hurts that the focus, as always, will be on Amber this entire time. I'm also mad that Dad ended up telling Amber after my parents decided last night not to. Their initial rationale was that it would just give her an additional reason to get drunk, which sounds about right to me.

God is our refuge and strength, an ever-present help in trouble (Psalm 46:1).

Journal Entry 10

I passed my final exam! It was pretty brutal, definitely the hardest final I've ever taken. My heart hurts that Mom and Dad both knew about today and didn't even check in. And of course, I immediately jump to the worst conclusion, assuming something happened with Amber and they're protecting me from it until my exam is completed. If nothing happened, I'm mad I wasted time worrying. If something did happen, I just added more stress. My heart is heavy. It's hard that my classmates have mentioned their parents asking about the test while I keep checking my phone with the hope of a new message. I know it's stupid, but it's been a really, really hard week and it would be nice for someone to check in on me.

Journal Entry 11

I'm supposed to go to Texas for Christmas, and it's made me extremely anxious. I thought it was reasonable to mention my boundaries and expectation that Amber respect them during my time in Texas to my dad. I thought talking about my plans to go to Houston or Dallas to get away from the house if Amber got out of control would make him say something like, "No, don't do that, we want to spend time with you" (especially since Amber lives with them and they see her daily). Instead, he said going to those places would be a good idea so I can get away. Why doesn't he want to see me? He even brought up that I would be home for over a month, and I corrected that it would only be a few weeks since I'm spending over a week visiting my best friend's family. I thought he would say something about missing me, but he sounded relieved. He's more worried about upsetting Amber than excited to spend time with me. That really hurts. It doesn't matter what I do or how I act. My time and relationship with my dad are solely reliant on Amber. My sister does more and more to destroy our family and, as a result, my dad becomes more and more enthralled with her. Meanwhile, the time spent on me is continually down-trending. He even mentioned that as soon as Amber is doing better, he wants to come visit me. So, basically, when hell freezes over he will come visit. I know my worth can't be found in my dad, but I have always admired him so much that it cuts deep not to have his recognition. Why am I not enough? Why am I not worth visiting? Why doesn't he want to spend time with me? Why is Amber more important than me? He says he's proud of me, and I know he thinks that he needs to focus on Amber because he thinks I'll be fine. But I'm not fine. I'm not even okay. He talks about Amber needing to get help before she realizes she needs to stop drinking, but she doesn't take her meds and doesn't do anything. If I stopped taking my meds, I would be suicidal again, but no one knows I've ever gotten to that point because no one knows the struggles my brain has constantly faced.

Prayer for the night: Lord, you are my peace and serenity. I pray for my upcoming trip to Texas where I'll be arriving short on sleep and needing to be at my peak. I pray for peace so deep that I authentically want to be there to help and listen. I pray for a patient heart to not argue but instead to be filled with love. I pray for my insecurities, that they will fade as I find myself in you. Lord, I pray I would define myself by you and your standards so that I would be able to see things more clearly and correctly.

Journal Entry 12

I need validation, and I know a big chunk of that needs to come from trusting God with my worth, but I just feel so down. If alcoholism affects so many people, then why can everyone else deal with it? Why does it impact me so much? Why am I considering going to Texas, the place I've been avoiding? I'm terrified to go there yet I feel guilty for avoiding it.

Journal Entry 13

Dad is trying to schedule meetings in the Denver area next year so that he has a reason to come stop by and see me. He mentioned this and I know that he meant it in a good way. However, the message I take away from this is that I'm not enough by myself. It makes it seem like he needs another reason to come to Colorado instead of just coming because he wants to see me. If I'm only a secondary reason to visit, then why do I want him to come so badly? I know if I ever told him this he would schedule a trip out of guilt, at least a part of me thinks that, but another part of me knows that if Amber had anything going on he would just call and say it was faulty thinking on my part.

I also know I could talk to my mom about it, but it would just start a fight between them, and they are already struggling enough as it is.

I don't know why tonight is so hard. Usually, I can handle things a lot more stoically, but I'm a blubber baby currently. Maybe it's because, through these past few weeks, I haven't had a good hard cry. I've shed some tears, but for the most part, I've stayed numb. Maybe it's all just leaking out tonight. Or maybe these recent realizations hurt me more than my sister's manipulation did.

Journal Entry 14

I think I must be jealous of Amber, otherwise it wouldn't bother me that my dad said one sentence in a text about her. So I guess the real question is, what is wrong with my heart at the moment causing me to feel so vulnerable?

Journal Entry 15

I had such a great devotion time this morning, it was one of my first truly quiet mornings in a while. I know it was preparing me for the call my dad was about to make. Basically, he wanted to tell me I needed to be the "bigger" person and help my sister when I come to visit. I have to admit, it really hurts that I'm pulling strings to be off of work so that I can visit him, yet he's still focused on my sister.

He recently canceled plans to attend my cousin's wedding because my sister decided she wasn't going, and she couldn't be trusted home alone. I was really looking forward to spending time with him there. At one point he said, "Wow, has it really been since Christmas?" which I'm sure was just an expression, but how does he not realize how long I've been gone? Why is it only my sister who gets prioritized? I don't want to be jealous, but it hurts, it really does. He's my dad, too, so why am I not enough just to be me? Why is it important to me that I be prioritized?

I'm going to need a lot of help this coming weekend. That one short phone call drained me and that was after a great devotion and a restful night of sleep. I have so many things going against me, it will only be by God's strength that I'm able to make it.

I think I'm looking at this wrong. I can't go into this weekend just trying to survive it. I need confidence in the Holy Spirit to be bold and have expectations that God will work through me.

I mean, after all, he is God. By underestimating him, I'm limiting his work. I want to be willing, hopeful, and patient. I want to be full of the fruits of the Spirit per Galatians 5:22–23: love, joy, peace, patience, kindness, goodness, faithfulness, gentleness, and self-control, so that my mind is in the right place.

Life as a Christian was meant to be an adventure. Am I willing to be humble enough to lose the battle this weekend so that God might win the war? Am I healthy enough to get mixed up with my family again? It hurts my heart to think of the words I'm about to hear that will forever be ingrained in my mind. I can sometimes brush off Amber, but when Dad says things to support her or seems disappointed in me, it hurts so much more. Am I willing to risk hurting him by telling him the pain he is causing me when I already worry about how he's coping? Really, that's what it comes down to. Would I rather live with resentment or potential guilt?

At church, we talked about Abraham and how God waited until the last possible moment to save his son. Am I willing to hold onto faith for Amber until we reach that point?

As for this weekend, am I more afraid to regret an opportunity to share my faith, or will I regret sacrificing my vulnerability and opening myself to truly horrible words that might be said to me? I think my biggest prayer should be for wisdom to know what is true of words and who I truly am.

Journal Entry 16

I hate that, even after setting boundaries and removing myself from her life, her addiction and habits still impact me. Mom is convinced she's on meth, which, to be honest, is probably accurate. But it sucks that, no matter what we do, she always comes up as a main topic. And I get it, she's what's on all our minds, but it would be nice to have a day that didn't revolve around her. I know that starts with my own mind, and not letting her control me, but I've got a way to go before I'm at that point.

I think I'm getting sick, which doesn't help, but I have a counseling session tomorrow that will be really good to help my mind heal. Also, I had a long talk with my sponsor tonight and that was good for my soul. God will get me through this.

Journal Entry 17

I read a poem once and I don't think I could do it justice to word it any more perfectly.

I am the other child.
The ok one.
I am the sober child.
The one on the sidelines.
I am the observer.
The one watching him slowly killing our parents.
I am the angry one.
The one who's pissed because he's destroying our family.
I am the sad one.
The one losing her first best friend.
I am the reassuring one.
The one holding her Momma as she cries.
I am the torn one.
The broken one trying to hold everyone together.
I am the confused one.
The one who wonders how we became so unimportant and invisible.
I am the other child.
The ok one.
—Author unknown[2]

2. Quoted in Frederiksen, "Sober Child," para. 5.

8

Anger

SHORT STORY

When I was little, I would sneak peeks at Amber's diary and try to find hidden secrets about her life. Honestly, the only thing I really cared about was her "love life." As much of a love life as a middle schooler had. As she grew up and started having committed relationships in high school, I switched from stealing her diary to hiding in corners and trying to get that perfect picture of the new couple locking lips. Honestly, it's kind of a miracle she never punched me. She had so many reasons to be angry with the brat that I could be, yet, instead, she taught me about grace through her actions. Of course, she would be upset when my snooping came to light, but she was quick to forgive and showed me so much mercy each time this happened. We shared a room, so it would have been easy for her to reciprocate my poor life choices. Instead, she chose to be an example to me and continued loving me throughout those growing years. I have learned so much from the lessons she showed me through her actions and the grace she offered me as I made many poor choices growing up.

SUMMARY

I get so angry that I want to scream, shout, kick, and punch everything around me. Unfortunately, after many attempts, none of this has made me feel better. I've tried exercise, journaling, talking, everything. I just have this constant rage inside of me that won't leave me alone. I'm constantly angry with every fiber of my being. I'm mad at my sister for putting us all in this situation. I'm furious with my parents for enabling her, for putting other people at risk by not throwing her keys away, and for prioritizing her. I'm mad that I can't focus because I'm so distracted. Worst of all, I'm mad at myself for not being able to do anything. I want to look forward to Christmas, I want to *want* to go home for Thanksgiving break. I just want life to be normal for a short amount of time, but that's never going to happen. When Amber chose alcohol over our family, she decided for all of us that our futures would shift. There's no going back, my forever is altered, and I'm angry that I didn't get a say. I've spent my fair share of time punching mirrors and screaming at pictures as memories became tinted with sadness. While not the healthiest way to manage anger, sometimes you can't keep it all inside.

JOURNALS

Journal Entry 1

I'm angry. I hate listening to friends talk about benign things and then acting as if life is crazy. I can't even add thoughts or stories that are calm because they would be too insane for people to try to comprehend. My life is a mess, so messy that I can't even share it when friends are talking about crazy stories. What does that mean?

Journal Entry 2

I'm so angry!!! It doesn't matter what happens, I'm just furious today. I don't want to laugh at jokes my professors make, I don't want people to correct me when I'm wrong, and I don't want to make small talk. I simply want to scream! The idea of punching something sounds great. I want to run full force and tackle someone to the ground. A game of football would be freaking amazing right now. But ugghhh!!!

I hate showing up to class on Monday morning and having to pretend like everything is the same as it was when I left on Friday. In some ways, I'm the same person. I sit in the same spot, I type the same notes, and, in some ways, everything is just as I left it. In other ways, my life is completely different, though. My family has changed, my normal has shifted yet again, and my future is altered more than it was on Friday. I thought I was okay, but I'm not, I'm simply taking longer to process. I've become better at denial. Or maybe I have gotten better, but not great yet. For example, I'm able to function this time, and I'm able to not break down in tears, but I am not able to go about as if nothing changed. It's like I've compartmentalized into drawers, but those drawers are too full to shut. As a result, they are all being blown and strewn about even though they are technically in their correct compartments. Maybe one day I'll get to the point where things don't impact me, but then again, how many more times do I have to go through this pain to get to that status? Is it worth it?

I should probably go to counseling. I know I'm not okay, but I think it would probably be more concerning if I was okay with everything that's happening. I think that might be comforting, or it might be really depressing that my life is so messed up, I can't decide. And back to counseling, I already know what I'll be told. Journal, take time to feel things, be kind to myself, and do things that are good like eating and exercising. In that sense, why pay money to be told what I already know? And I don't want to have to pay someone to listen to my drama. I want someone to care, I want someone who will tell me everything is going to be okay. However, that's another complicated part, it would be a lie if someone said everything would be okay. There is a higher chance things won't be than they will. How do you deal with a problem that likely has no solution, or at least no way to implement the solution, because it's out of your control?

I went to the gym over lunch, and I feel a lot better. I was able to get some of my anger out by running until I couldn't breathe. Later, I got a text from an Al-Anon friend about a new meeting in the Denver area. There is hope, and there is community, it just happens to be in areas I've never thought to look.

I turn on a lamp that barely lights the dark room. I close my eyes and start to pray. When I open my eyes, the room is bursting with light. I know there's science and adjusting and all that to explain it, but I love the symbolism of giving this situation to God, trusting him, and, suddenly, a dim room has light again.

This whole time I've been frustrated. I hate that my parents enable Amber, but I'm starting to realize how horrific it would be if they didn't have hope. After all, if they could give up on her then it sets the standard that they could also give up on me. Sure, it wouldn't be substances after seeing how much they destroy those around you. But the number of mistakes I make a day is incalculable, so I guess for the first time ever I'm grateful for the enabling that represents hope and love.

Journal Entry 3

Mom has been really depressed today. She later mentioned that she shouldn't check Amber's room because it only makes her sad and frustrated. I didn't say anything because this is all common sense. Nothing has changed, and nothing ever will if they keep enabling her. My parents are shocked every time Amber shows her alcoholism. I'm so frustrated that our lives are dictated by a constant focus on addition. I wish we could all just snap out of it and focus on the life going on around us. The struggle is, when your brain is saturated in the fears and traumas of addiction constantly, it's impossible to focus on anything else.

Journal Entry 4

I sit here angry that I can't get past a stupid memory from so many years ago. As the tears roll down my face, I finally realize that it has nothing to do with one memory. It's what that event represents. All the hurt, lies, and manipulation have never been more evident than on that specific trip.

Journal Entry 5

I'm so angry! I want to scream and shout and kick and punch and probably some other stuff too. The problem is I don't think that would make me feel better. I even went on a run this morning and that didn't perk me up. I'm angry with every fiber of my being.

I have so many things that I need to be doing but I just can't. I can barely get through life right now, much less add extra things to the plate. How am I supposed to keep up when I'm struggling just to go through the motions? I need a break to process the dumpster fire that is my reality. I need patience from people who think I'm just acting bratty or dramatic. I need encouragement from friends who don't know what's going on but hopefully can see that I'm struggling. I need people to be able to read my mind and support me in ways I can't even figure out to ask for. I need love from people who aren't my family because these people are who I'll turn to every time my biologics choose addiction over me.

Journal Entry 6

Jesus rebukes and disciplines because he loves us, it's different from punishment. Amber needs some freaking discipline in order to respect our parents. I need to get over my anger, it boils up in me and sets me on the edge constantly, so that's probably not healthy.

Journal Entry 7

I want to be there to support my mom and be strong enough that she can vent to me and lean on me. But as soon as she starts talking, I get so overcome by frustration. She commented tonight on the phone: "It's really tough, but I have my family to get me through." I don't want to get her through. I want her to go get professional help from a therapist so that I can enjoy my mom. I don't want to practice empathetic statements and listening skills every time we talk, I just want my mom.

I'll never have a life without addiction because no matter what happens, it will always haunt us all.

Journal Entry 8

It's funny that through anonymity we find who we truly are. It's almost like we have to forget who we are in order to clearly see what's been there the entire time. I realized today that my fears were totally irrational, yet simultaneously completely valid. I think that's what makes them so frustrating and terrifying. If they were rational, I could at least know how to avoid them or protect myself against them. But their irrationality makes them a hundred times more potent. I guess that's probably a good perspective or insight or something.

My mom is coming to visit in February, and I truly am excited. However, I'm a little hurt that she once again based the arrangements around my sister. My dad was supposed to have meetings in Florida, so as a result she was going to reschedule the trip that she promised to take and stop letting Amber dictate her life and her schedule. However, since my dad was going to be out of town it immediately made her realize she didn't mean the words she said. Indeed, she was going to do exactly what she swore not to do. My dad ended up not going on his trip, so it all worked out. However, I can't help but feel almost betrayed that she once again prioritized my sister just because she required more attention. I find myself struggling more with my parents as I struggle less with their addicted child. Maybe I am just passing the blame and pooling it in different buckets, or maybe it's something that I haven't thought of or can't comprehend yet. Whatever the case, I'm excited to continue counseling Friday and get back to that rhythm. I think having consistent support will really help my stability and focus for this coming semester.

Journal Entry 9

Some days I'm mad. Not in a throw-stuff-punch-people kind of way. More like I'm tilting on the side of a firecracker and everyone walking by is a potential flame. I can barely hold myself together, so any simple inconvenience is both exhausting and devastating. I don't have the patience or compassion to function as an adult should. *That's both my responsibility and not my fault all at the same time.*

Journal Entry 10

I thought I was relating to Mom yesterday, but I had forgotten about the anger piece when I feel I know what's best and no one listens to me. I don't have a voice in this situation, yet my voice will forever be impacted by what happens.

Journal Entry 11

I'm furious! I'm just so sick of all of this. UGHHHHHHHH, maybe I was in denial before when I was just sad, or maybe there's just been too many hits and I can't take it. Either way, I just want to scream, jump, or kick a board in half.

Journal Entry 12

Something else I hate is the stigma of addiction. If my sister was in the hospital, typically our entire church would be praying for her, people would be bringing food, and everyone would be compassionate. In this case, my parents haven't told anyone. They want to protect her privacy as much as they can. When I bring it up I'm told, "It's not my story to tell," so my typical support system is cut off. It doesn't matter that this is life or death and that hospitals are scary and unpredictable no matter why you are admitted. We are alone. More than that, even if they did tell people, *no one brings casseroles for addicts.* No one comes over with hugs and love because of mental health and the trauma of watching someone slowly kill themselves in front of you. It's the most isolated I've ever felt, I just want a hug. I just want support. I just want someone to understand.

9

Confusion

We took a family trip to Hawaii after I graduated high school, and Amber graduated college. I remember so many times looking at each other after one of us would do something totally boneheaded and realizing that we had both graduated at the top of our classes yet simultaneously had no common sense. Before that trip, we both wanted to do something rebellious, so I dyed my hair black with blue highlights while she went for Little Mermaid Red. We had both attended schools with strict dress codes so dying our hair "unnatural colors" felt like we were really living on the edge. We made a lot of fashion and life choices when we were young that, looking back, weren't the brightest, but as long as we did them together, it didn't matter what anyone else thought. There was a steep learning curve where we both had some misguided beauty sense, but that's what sisters are for, making mistakes and growing together. Before she left for college we shared a bathroom, and in the mornings we would give each other fashion advice. Amber was always so talented at doing makeup and some days she would teach me tips and tricks. I was always conflicted about being so impressed with Amber's talent yet wondering why she covered herself in products when she was already the prettiest person I knew. It always made me feel so mature when she would teach me things and at times even do my eye makeup for me. I wanted to be just like her, and anyway that I could get closer I would pounce on.

SUMMARY

When everything you know becomes out of control, it's like your homeostasis is completely changed. Up becomes down, the sky becomes green while the grass changes to blue. Things become so messed up that there's no longer a right and a wrong, there's just a messy normal. You become so afraid that you hide behind a smile and then simultaneously become frustrated when no one realizes that you are struggling. You become relieved, which makes you feel guilty and then you start to feel hope which makes you terrified. There are no longer individual emotions because each feeling is associated with a bag of complex future associations.

JOURNALS

Journal Entry 1

I'm watching soap opera YouTube clips because it's like a form of therapy. I feel like my life isn't the only one that's messed up and crazy when I see their stories. It makes me feel like a part of some sort of weird, messed-up group who gets it. Even though these people are fake and scripted, I feel like they understand what it's like to live in constant chaos.

Journal Entry 2

I just got off the phone with my dad. He called to make sure I knew what was going on, which I appreciate. *He still has hope, I don't know if I pity or envy him for that.*

My mind is full. Full of questions that no one can answer. Full of memories singing in the background. Full of anger at the reality I live in, and dashed with hope that I try not to get attached to. I can't count the number of times I've gone through old pictures to reflect on good times. These sessions usually end with me questioning what was actually going on in the photos, but at least for a bit, it's comforting nostalgia. I even tried watching *Gossip Girl*[1] last night because it was a show Amber and I used to watch together. I got through half of an episode before losing focus. It was worth a shot if it meant being able to reconnect with some part of her; even one minute of having a sister again is worth the effort.

Journal Entry 3

Amber called today and I know I need to have patience and love for her, but I really struggle. That's where God comes in, he is so much greater than each part of me. I started praying about identity and how my sister and I could be so alike yet so different. Also about how to define who my sister is or, for that matter, who I am. Is it simply a conglomeration of events that have happened, or are we something before things happen to us?

The conclusion I came to is . . . we need identities like we need time. It organizes and makes an infinite thing understandable. If the past is stripped away, we have nothing to compare the present to, and without a comparison we can't adequately judge good from bad. So, in a way, we are the sum of experiences and events. But that's not necessarily a bad thing. Everything that happens dictates how we see right, wrong, evil, forgiveness, etc. We grow into independent beings who are not set to be defined by our identities; rather, we get to use those identities to shape our future. God is so good.

1. Schwartz and Savage, *Gossip Girl*.

Journal Entry 4

I realized today that I'm terrified of anyone knowing the real me. I look back to a time when I was asked to give a quote and I made someone else say one because the idea of others reading something personal was terrifying. I look at memories of "get-to-know-you games" when we have to share a random fact and I always say I have a pet fish. It's because I'm absolutely terrified of letting anyone become close to me or know anything personal. I'm so good at putting on a front and living my pretend life, that I can't fathom letting people know anything that's really happening. I think it's a mix of irrationality and the idea that if I open the door a crack it will continue to swing open. It's ironic because I think I'm proud of what I've accomplished and feel very privileged to have had an interesting life of overcoming obstacles. I think maybe I should be okay sharing some things. Maybe.

Journal Entry 5

I feel foggy, like I'm so overstimulated that I can't focus on any one thing. It's like my mind is running away from its burdens and as long as it doesn't stop then all is well. I'm trying to figure out the line between trusting God and denial.

I feel like I did months ago, where I think I'm relatively unaffected by addiction, but then I notice I'm on edge and getting easily frustrated over pointless things. For example, in class today we wrote assignments and then we were supposed to have two classmates correct them. I felt deeply hurt that those classmates found anything wrong with mine, which was literally the assignment. But it made me realize how much I'm struggling with things that wouldn't typically bother me. I keep thinking of this as a phase when in reality I think my life has shifted. I don't know what to make of that, but at least it's something.

Journal Entry 6

My pain feels invalidated, it seems like I should be able to continue my normal life since I'm "unaffected." After all, how long can I let something that's out of my control dictate my life? Maybe it's time to move on . . . but how does someone "move on" from their family? I love my family and I love my life. It's not something I want to just forget and disappear. But I also can't let it rule my every thought and I don't know how to make a compromise at the moment. It all overlaps too much in my mind.

I do think it's possible, though, to one day be okay. This is a huge victory from where I was previously. I think between friends, extended family, and Al-Anon, I might eventually be okay.

Journal Entry 7

I need to take responsibility. Just like I want my sister to admit her hurt, I need to be strong enough to stand alone and admit the hurt I have caused in all of this. If I put all my happiness, excitement, and comfort in other people then I am not truly being me. And if I make my family live false lives to protect me from hurt, that's not fair to them. If everything I do is based on the reactions of others, then I have turned into the problem that I face when dealing with my sister. If I do something intentionally hurtful or even if something I do causes significant distress in an understandable situation, then I should take ownership and apologize. However, one of the big battles of addiction is that nothing is rational. So, the idea of me fighting to make peace and constantly overthinking how to keep everyone happy is in itself impossible, because an irrational system cannot have a rational solution.

Journal Entry 8

I want to be alone; I don't want anyone to know what's really going on. Then again, I want everyone to know what's happening. I want people to realize that my world is being destroyed and I'm forced to function as if everything is fine. I want to make an announcement that says, "Be nice to me," "Have grace," "Be patient," and "I am really struggling and can't handle the normal dose of life today." Rationally I know that my classmates are going through things too. Many of them have struggles that are equally earth-shattering, but to me, this addiction is all-encompassing and I'm incapable of seeing their issues. This is incredibly ironic since I expect them to notice my destruction.

10

Broken

SHORT STORY

When we were young and living in Minnesota, my parents built a shed that my siblings and I turned into a clubhouse for "top secret" meetings of a group we affectionately called the Bumblebee Spy Club. It's funny because I can't think of a single mystery we tried to solve, but some of my favorite memories are secret handshakes, hidden messages, and pretending to save the world together. We were a strong unit and it felt like as long as we worked together, we could fix anything. There's something so special about being part of a group and knowing that even if you mess up, the other people in your unit will lift you up and support you. Even though I was four years younger (which is about twenty years in the kid world) Amber still empowered me to be a leader of the group and instilled confidence in me. It's one of the traits that helps me get through each season of trials.

SUMMARY

Sometimes life is so unexplainably messed up that you know you need help, but it feels too exhausting to reach out. The world becomes too heavy to carry. There's the desire for someone to tell you everything will be okay, battling with the frustration of not wanting to hear any more lies. It's the times you need help but aren't sure who to turn to. With friends, their primary reactions to hard times are to call home. But home doesn't feel like home when it's the cause of your stress. During these periods it's hard to feel anything but broken. It can be as if so many pieces of you are spread across the ground that putting them back together feels impossible. Just finding the tiny shreds that once made up your life seems overwhelming. But no matter how destroyed you get, every piece is still present and able to be put back in place. In fact, some cultures celebrate brokenness and the way that this creates beauty. The Japanese practice of kintsugi highlights this best. People outline the cracks in gold to embrace the imperfections and celebrate what makes them unique. It is so easy to hide our flaws from the world, but each flaw is beauty and growth hidden by pain.

JOURNALS

Journal Entry 1

Something said at Al-Anon that stood out was the question, *How free do you want to be?* I think that's the whole Al-Anon program tied up in a nutshell. You can work it as much or as little as you want and be as open and vulnerable as you want. It really comes down to getting what you put into it. If I want to be free, I need to go all in and be okay with feeling uncomfortable with growing pains along the way.

Journal Entry 2

I decided to call my mom when I got back; I found out that Amber was going through withdrawal and was so sick of it she decided to check herself out of the hospital. My mom is fully ready to kick her out of the house, but my dad isn't. I imagine that must be really challenging. Now if only I could compartmentalize this along with everything else about life right now.

Journal Entry 3

I'm not okay. I'm sad, broken, hurt, isolated, hopeless, scared, furious, empty, and disappointed. I can't concentrate on tasks that people are counting on me to do. I want to be okay, but my life is constantly teetering and waiting for something else to go wrong. I am so easily upset, small things happen and they make me want to cry. Life is just so messed up. I'm hurting so much, and I don't see the future getting any better. My hope has dwindled. I want someone to hug me and tell me they are there for me and that they can tell how exhausted I am. Tell me that I'm doing a good job and that I will be okay. However, simultaneously I don't want to hear lies, and I don't know if any of that is true. My heart is broken. I'm broken. I need help but I don't know where to start.

Journal Entry 4

I'm stressed, I'm scared, I'm exhausted, I'm confused, I'm hurt. Should I bother to share my opinions since mom already agrees and dad already disagrees? Is it better to think my opinion doesn't matter, or to think it does? What's the balance between validation of myself and support for my parents?

Journal Entry 5

The world is just too much sometimes. My shoulders continually get crunched by the pressure. There are so many times when I don't feel strong enough to withstand it anymore. I start to question why no one can see that I'm not okay. Is everyone too preoccupied, or am I really that good of an actress? These times make me want to curl up and let the world pass by for a bit. It can all become too much, all the time, never ending. This life is a constant cycle of wondering what explosion is coming next. It's not highs and lows, it's lows and bombs that disintegrate the lows to create new lows that weren't previously fathomable.

Journal Entry 6

There are so many things I attempt to help keep my attitude positive. I can't count the trips I've taken to the dog park. Something about the combination of the fresh air and sweet doggos all around should make anyone feel a bit more chipper. Hours have been spent journaling, praying, exercising, listening to music and self-help books, along with pretty much every possible option that my therapist has recommended. However, there comes a time when even with a million coping strategies, a person's heart simply breaks.

Journal Entry 7

The Country Music Association Awards are airing tonight. I can't help but think of the time Amber and I went together, and the year before, when we went to the CMA Christmas taping. I remember her getting drunk, which I didn't think anything of at the time, but now I look back and wonder if I should have been more concerned. Could I have prevented anything? Would it have just made our relationship more distant earlier?

Journal Entry 8

My equilibrium has been shifted to living in a hurricane. Calm, sunny beaches have lost their appeal. Sure, I dream about them, but when I'm actually stepping out into the sand, I start spinning in circles because it returns my body to homeostasis. Healthy or not, that's the place I relate to as home, or at least the place my brain feels balanced.

Journal Entry 9

I find it ironic that multiple older adults have felt the need to mention that people my age haven't lived long enough to know true trauma. I don't even know where to begin with this idea that pain and heartbreak can somehow be nonexistent until you reach a certain age. I'm aware that I haven't suffered nearly as much trauma as some people half my age or people twice my age. Sure, being alive longer gives you more time to experience pain. However, that doesn't mean tragedy is isolated into an older age bracket. It's honestly ironic that a "young person" needs to explain to them that trauma does not directly correlate with age.

11

Pain

SHORT STORY

One year when Amber was living in Florida for college, it didn't
work with her schedule to come home for Thanksgiving. Instead,
my parents flew me out to spend it with her so she wouldn't be
alone. We had such a special day getting dressed in cute outfits
and taking pictures all over her town. We got wrapped up in the
day as she showed me around her favorite spots. We didn't realize
until late afternoon that we hadn't made any plans for the actual
Thanksgiving dinner. Once we made this realization, we rushed
to the only open store and browsed for anything similar to turkey.
After finding out how long it would take to make any sort of actual
dinner, we settled for sushi and a pizza. We had an absolute blast
eating our picnic on her living room floor and watching *Gilmore
Girls.*[1] Amber is the one who first introduced me to *Gilmore Girls.*
For years we would quote funny lines and random parts to each
other anytime we could possibly fit the comments in. Even in an
ironic sense, if we could make it happen, we would add the refer-
ence to show we had something in common and understood each

1. Sherman-Palladino, *Gilmore Girls.*

81

other on a deeper level than those around us. Between the unique meal and countless quotes of the weekend, it will forever be one of my favorite memories.

SUMMARY

Pain is a word that means so many different things to so many different people, yet the basic principle is the same. We may not have identical experiences or choose similar adjectives, but we all understand the fundamental hurt. There's no way to describe the exhaustion and stress from the drama and unknowns that accompany loving an alcoholic. It's nearly impossible to explain why it hurts to have your parents too distracted to realize how deeply you are struggling while concurrently fully understanding why they can't be present. Then there's the hurt of wishing you could do more and wondering why you aren't enough of a reason for your addict to quit. The turmoil of wondering why you aren't trustworthy and loving enough for your addict to tell you the truth instead of filling each conversation with continuous lies. It's the conflicting feelings of wanting to be strong and putting up a façade that you are okay while also desperately wishing someone would realize how broken you are and how deeply you are struggling just to keep breathing. It's wanting a week where life is okay but knowing that may never come because even if things are calm, there will still be the worry of what's around the corner. It's wanting to grow stronger from the experience and wanting to be inspirational, yet being too tired and hurt by it all to form any thoughts. As a result, you feel isolated, broken, and hurt. There's no better way to say it than being in pain.

JOURNALS

Journal Entry 1

My heart breaks as I look at the picture on my desk from my brother's wedding. Even then, Amber was an alcoholic, but she was still functional. When I compare the wedding picture to the photos from this week, I can't even recognize her. If I hadn't followed the progression, I wouldn't associate her as the same person. As much as I know the stats and doubt Amber will ever get better, there's always that piece of hope that gives a tiny glimmer to my sad eyes. I wear a necklace every day and it's a big heart with a tiny heart hanging from it. Unless you are up close staring at my neck, you would never see the little heart that hangs by the side. I think that's how my heart's hope is right now. It's still there, but only visible in the most important times.

Journal Entry 2

How long does something simply impact you before it starts defining you? My therapist says it's okay for emotions to bubble up at random times even if I can't explain it, but if every event in my life continued to alter my emotions, then wouldn't I be a circus of spiraling feelings? Are we simply affected by the most pertinent event? Does that mean most recent or most impactful? Because, on the one hand, the more recent the event the more feelings tend to bubble up. However, I just ate lunch and, sure that brings up some emotions if I think deeply about it, but as I type about my family I swear I can physically feel pieces of my heart floating away. The pain is so real and so continual that I can't fathom a day when I look back on this and smile at the building God was doing in my life. I know that God has been showing me signs that a big storm is coming, but I feel like I've been in the ocean these past few years. Wave after wave crashes into me, I finally find a lifeboat and catch my breath, just to get thrown back in. Maybe that's the issue, maybe my entire problem is that I'm trying to fight the waves. I'm doing everything humanly possible to keep getting oxygen to my body. All I can focus on is trying to survive. Whereas if I would simply release my control and trust that there will be a whale to swallow me up, I could relax and be free to do what God has been trying to point me toward. Wow, that's crazy, hmmmm. I wonder if God ever feels like a kindergarten teacher who tells his pupils over and over and over about how to live, yet it takes us months to finally grasp these simple concepts that he has spelled out for us hundreds of times.

Lord, what do you have planned for my life? I now realize that I have been stubbornly fighting against your unfailing grip and for that, I apologize. I ask for your help to release my tight grasp on this aspect that I have no control over. I pray that I will be able to fully trust in you and know that you are going to use me for your glory as well as do everything in order that your will for my life might be completed. Lord, I'm nervous but I'm ready. Scratch that, I'm nervous and I'm ready. The two aren't contradictory, they simply both exist in my mind. My nervousness will gradually go away, but, for now, I trust you over my fears and struggles. I trust you with it all.

Journal Entry 3

I spent two hours today with an overdose patient who, for all intents and purposes, could have been Amber; my efforts were wasted. My heart is still recovering from imagining this possible future and realizing again how devastating addiction is. It's so sad. I wish I had anywhere near the eloquent words this emotion deserves, but all I can come up with right now is *sad*. The truth is, there will never be a word deep enough to describe the absolute horrors of addiction. It's simply outside of the bounds of language. Words can only go so far; at some point, emotion transcends that.

Journal Entry 4

I was talking to a mentor today and she mentioned she felt really bad for my parents. As a parent herself, she could explain how giving an addict money logically was harmful in the long run but if it means your child will be alive for another day, then it's worth it. Parents will do absolutely anything for their kids so the inability to fix them is excruciating. I've heard this in similar ways before, but somehow talking with her made me feel real empathy for what my parents must be going through. I always compare things to me and how deeply I've been impacted, but I haven't been able to look around and truly see other people's pain until tonight. I feel like I can look around the world tomorrow and not simply glance over the same objects that I was blinded to today.

Journal Entry 5

If you have a sprained ankle, it takes time to heal. Just because you have continued pain doesn't mean you aren't improving. I may require more time to heal, and that's okay.

Journal Entry 6

I turned on a movie to help me focus on studying. I know that sounds counterproductive, but once my body reaches a certain point of stress, I have to distract my brain enough to vaguely focus on different topics. I happened to choose one of those cheesy Christmas movies about royalty, a palace, and all that romantic stuff. I had seen it a million times and thought it would be the perfect background distraction with lots of colors but not too engaging. At first, all was fine and dandy, but at one point a character goes off on her own and everyone begins running around screaming her name. This is probably a good time to mention that the character's name is Amber, so all I hear is, "Amber where are you?"[2] and it hits way too close to home. There's a similar scene constantly playing in my mind: I search for where the sister I love and grew up with has disappeared to.

Journal Entry 7

I'm watching an episode of *7th Heaven*[3] about a boy dropping a joint that one of the main characters hid in his pocket at school.

2. Zamm, *Christmas Prince.*
3. Beaumont, "Who Knew."

The whole point was that he never even did it, but his parents didn't give him a chance to talk or explain the situation. What really stuck out to me, though, was when his younger brother lost all respect for him when he thought drugs were happening, and when the sisters talked about how the parents wouldn't be able to trust him again. All I can think about is Amber and how I don't think I'll ever be able to trust her again. It's kind of sad that the TV show is about pot, which isn't even illegal anymore, and I had the thought while watching it, "If only Amber just did marijuana." What a messed-up situation life continues to be.

Journal Entry 8

This is alcoholism . . . sitting here crying in my bed instead of laughing with friends in their car talking about crushes and exciting life events. I decided to go to our class Friendsgiving tonight and I made the mistake of driving with friends because they all said they were okay with leaving early. I know they were having a good time, but what they don't understand is that I literally don't have it in me to stay any longer than my short fuse can take. It was a typical get-together where everyone brought food and drinks. It's not fair to friends that I am hypersensitive around alcohol, but it physically pains me to see so many people drinking in excess when alcohol has destroyed the family I love.

12

Fear of Hope

SHORT STORY

Our family would burn our piles of leaves at the end of each fall. My siblings and I would make "masks" out of plastic cups and wear safety goggles so that we could pretend to be firefighters. We spent countless nights running in circles around the burn piles and pretending to protect our house from the flames. We would run and scream until the smoke would eventually get into our lungs and we would end up inside laughing and feeling like superheroes who had just braved devastating wildfires. We would consider it another successful day protecting our house from a very "dangerous," tiny, well-controlled fire in the backyard. It's funny because my parents were the ones with the rakes and doing the actual fire control, yet these were some of our proudest young moments growing up. It was one of the many times that Amber showed me how to have courage and be brave even when the threat only felt like it was real.

SUMMARY

I will admit I'm scared. Every time I get to a place of peace, my world crashes apart. All I can think about when life calms down for a day is that a tornado must be headed for me. With so many catastrophes, the idea of hope is terrifying. The mere thought that things are currently okay creates fear because it means the other shoe is that much closer to dropping. There's no longer a life of peace. Instead, it feels like if I'm prepared for the worst, things aren't as disappointing when everything falls apart for the hundredth time. Being able to protect one's heart, even a small amount, seems to be worth the energy spent.

JOURNALS

Journal Entry 1

I Skyped a friend last night and told her things seemed to be okay with my family. Today I found out my parents have both booked tickets because Amber has spiraled yet again. It's crazy how fast things change. Mom will fly there while I'm in Texas for a break from school. I know mom feels bad that I'm coming home to visit them, and she will miss my time there. I really don't feel cheated or angry, honestly what hurts is the reality of how broken Amber is.

We learned in church today that, in Romans 12, when it says a *test* it's talking about a time where things matter. What matters right now is that I give my discouragement, frustration, hurt, and sadness to God. He's the only one who gets it. He's the only one who can't empathy block because he completely understands the tiny details that even I can't comprehend.

I'm listening to a song called "You're Gonna Be Ok"[1] that is really comforting, this is a good time to meet with God. I know I also need community, but right now I need to first lean on God.

I keep thinking I'll wake up and this year will have been a nightmare, but then I realize it's unlikely this will be complete in

1. Brian & Jenn Johnson, "You're Gonna Be OK."

a year. The shattered fragments of this year will haunt our lives forever. However, a lot of good things happened this year too. It's easy to be discouraged and hurt, but it's not fair to let the pain overshadow all the good.

I'm going to be okay (repeat, repeat).

Journal Entry 2

I think I feel hopeful. This terrifies me.

Journal Entry 3

There was something said at Al-Anon about acknowledging the obstacle or hard event but not being angry or casting blame. I don't know that I'm there; actually, I know I'm not there, but at least I have a goal. I now have glimpses of the clarity I want. For instance, when I talked with someone and was able to explain not taking mom and dad personally, and about them living constantly on the edge about to spill over. It's not anger about it, I mean sure it sucks and I have my "poor-me" moments, but it's just a fact like a defining characteristic. Not good or bad, it is simply a thing I can either accept or resent.

Journal Entry 4

I just had a great talk with my sponsor. She differentiated hope from expectation for me, which was really helpful. I have been pretty outspoken, without a filter, about the bleak outlook of this disease, and it's good to be reminded that it's possible to overcome it. *I am able to have hope that Amber will get better while not putting my expectations on her.*

Journal Entry 5

Today was amazing. I feel like I can focus on classes and, even more, I want to learn. I have the craving for knowledge that I had until addiction overshadowed all else. I've been so caught up in everything that I forgot how amazing knowledge is. It's ironic because I was so focused on learning everything I could about alcoholism and Amber that I forgot how and why I wanted to learn. For the first time in years I am not just able to focus on school but I enjoy it. I love the knowledge and how our body works so intricately to function properly. I'm amazed at the little beauties that I haven't appreciated in years. Life is really good and, until I was writing this, I hadn't even thought about the fact that the statement "life is good" terrifies me because it means a catastrophe is about to happen. I think, at least for a moment or two, I can forget about the future and enjoy the present.

I talked at Al-Anon tonight about the shift of setting a boundary with Amber and how it finally allowed me to give things over to God instead of trying to bargain and convince him to do things my way. I was so narcissistic before, I wanted control and to be able to fix things. Now I emotionally line up with my logical brain that knows I can't fix anything and everything is in the hands of God. I've never felt more peaceful and joyful. God is so good.

Journal Entry 6

I was flipping through old journals tonight and I opened a page from when I was living in Nicaragua and a friend told me that it was okay not to be strong and to cry. She told me "if you don't let the tears out, they remain in you and that's how you become hard." I can't think of anything more true or fitting. God has been showing me over and over this week that it's okay to ask people for help and that it's okay not to be okay and to be weak sometimes. I'm a little bit terrified of what that means because God never teaches a lesson for kicks and giggles. There's always a reason. Does this mean a hard season is coming? I don't feel like I've had more than a week off of hard seasons in years, but this week was a refreshing wave of relief and encouragement to stagger through the next wave. I'd like to say I will stand tall and mightily fight, but I think realistically it's going to look more like a stagger as I try my best to survive another blow. Maybe this is all me making connections and putting things together that aren't really there. Maybe God was trying to point these things out to me previously and I'm just super late to the party so I'm getting the memo late that was meant to comfort me in my trials. I can hope that's the case, yet I fear a tsunami is coming to wreck what the earthquake has left standing.

Journal Entry 7

My sister could have easily died tonight. The only reason she didn't must be that God has a purpose for her life. The other night I had this vivid image of Amber in a casket. It terrified me since I've never had that vision before. I know death is an option, but I naturally block it out of my mind. I remember praying and I can't help but wonder if she was actually dying at the time I was thinking and praying for her. Did God allow me to experience that so that I could pray for her? He saved her that night I have no doubt. Maybe he let me be a part of that, which is pretty special. Or maybe it was God showing me what I have to be grateful for and how easy it could be to lose Amber.

What would my life look like today if Amber died instead of my dad showing up to help her? Instead of missing work because I'm sick, I would be missing work because of funeral planning. It all seems so surreal that this could even be my life. I often think that I've over-dramatized things or made them seem worse in my head, but in reality, life is just completely and utterly messed up. I want to talk about it, but at the same time, I'm so overwhelmed that I can't even process everything I found out tonight. I knew things were messy, but everything is just so bleak.

On one hand, the fact that Amber is in a rehab facility gives me a glimmer of hope that I haven't felt in a long time. Then again, the events that led her there are terrifying and I can't help but wonder if she actually wants to be there/is willing to get help, or is this going to be a huge expense for my parents that doesn't lead to anything?

Journal Entry 8

How do I wrap my head around the fact that Amber might actually die soon? I need to work on processing all of this to try and make sense of it in my head. It's like the idea is so farfetched that I can't even find parameters to fit it into.

I've been thinking a lot lately about how so many people overdose right after rehab because they forget they no longer have their tolerance built up, so it's this constant war of trying to have hope and trying not to be terrified that this could actually cause her to die. Then again, she likely would have died if she wasn't in this rehab center. And yet she still needs to hit rock bottom. I honestly can't think of any options lower than where she has been other than death. It's almost scary how factual I can be about this because of all the times it's played over in my head and the hours I've spent trying to look for any other options at all. It will never be over, at least while I am still on this earth. It's always going to be a pain in my heart and a struggle of my mind.

Journal Entry 9

Mom said Amber called today and said they should sell all her stuff to pay for rehab. She also apparently asked for a picture of me and wanted my address. I'm devastated. Right now, I'm safe. I'm mourning the loss of our relationship, but I'm protected. I know a letter will hurt me no matter what it states. If it says horrible things directly or has implications filled with guilt, I won't be able to simply pretend I never read it. Logic won't be powerful enough to heal my broken heart. However, if she writes kind words then I'm stuck in the position of either being the person who won't forgive/ isn't there, or I let her back into my life and watch it crumble all over again. I'm finally in a healthy place and I know this process of destroying me will begin as soon as I open the door, even a crack. I guess maybe I could say something along the lines of being hurt and only wanting her sober, I don't know.

I don't want to deal with this. I'm so over addiction. Why can't it ever end? I can't imagine living the rest of my life with the battles that are to come.

Also, why is Amber writing? Mom thinks she's working on the steps and needs to make amends, but she hasn't even been in the program for two weeks so there is no way she's on that step if she's actually doing them. My assumption is she's treating it like the majority of new members. Running through the steps and racing to be cured. That's not how it works. I wish it were that simple.

I feel a glimmer of hope and it makes me shake with fear. I just had an image of me being at Al-Anon and being able to share about having a recovered alcoholic in my life. I could be one of the lucky ones, but I can't bear to dream. It hurts too much when it all crashes down.

Journal Entry 10

I've been watching a lot of Disney movies lately. I think it's the idea of a happy ending that intrigues me. I like knowing that no matter how messed up everything gets, the ending will always be happy. I like to think that even as messed up as my family currently is, there's a chance that we will also have a happy ending. I really hope that's not just for movies, but if it is, at least I get a glimmer.

13

Support

SHORT STORY

While we lived in Minnesota, gymnastics was a passion that Amber and I shared. She was always so much better than me, and I admired her talent and dedication. I remember thinking she was going to go to the Olympics and being convinced that she had the skills to do anything she set her mind to. During the summers we would spend our days at a local university where we would practice all day and then get a ride home from one of the coaches. I remember looking forward to lunch because it was a time when we would sit in the fresh air and talk about life while eating our daily tuna fish and crackers. She would teach me and encourage me after hard workout sessions when I was discouraged. Then, driving home we would play card games and talk about whatever happened to be on our minds. I learned so much about dedication, motivation, and teamwork from that time with her. She showed me what hard work could accomplish and how important it is to have the support of loved ones beside you.

SUMMARY

It was *Grey's Anatomy* where Christina says, "The one thing about being weak is it gives your friends a chance to catch you."[1]

I never fully appreciated my friends until this trial. Call me cliché, but these are the people who ultimately are getting me through. The ones who check on me, cry with me, and assure me I'm not crazy no matter how insane I feel. These comforters who listen for hours on the phone when yet another bomb has devastated my world. My friends are my rocks who take me on hikes to calm down, let me yell at them for doing stupid things that wouldn't bother a sane human, and most of all, lean into me when I cry because I can't handle it anymore. They have taken me from feeling despair to being able to remember what hope feels like. It's not an instant fix, I'm still messed up beyond understanding, but I can at least imagine being okay again.

It's funny because I always think of places like Bible school or church as places for deep relationships, and, indeed, they thrive there, but I've felt support in more areas of my life recently than ever before. I guess it's God's way of showing me he is present in every situation. God knew I needed these people in my life to help me through these days.

My extended family has also been amazing. Particularly my aunts who I have become much closer to in the past few years. They are the ones who cheer me up and know when I'm struggling and check in and send extra prayers during those moments. Life is impossible at times, but they stick by me through it all. One of the beautiful things about this trial has been finding the incredible people who I took for granted and overlooked before.

1. Stanzler, "Deny, Deny, Deny."

JOURNALS

Journal Entry 1

I'm reading a book called *The Search for Significance* by Robert McGee that talks about how we don't have to blame someone. I can be mad at addiction, but I don't have to figure out who or what caused it. I've been trying to figure it out for so long so that I can stop blaming the other things and really, it's okay not to know. I know that I hate addiction and what it's done to my family, so why hate more? Isn't a tiny bit of hate more than enough? Hmmm.

Journal Entry 2

I have the best friends. So many of my close friends reached out in different, special ways this week. One took me to the dog park and coffee, another went on a hike with me, a different one checked in and validated my many emotions, while the other showed her constant strong support by holding me up when I mentally broke down. They have become my family through this all. Things might potentially be looking up. I don't want to get my hopes up, but I think things might be okay this week. I'm also meeting with my sponsor tomorrow, so that will be a good way to talk things through.

Journal Entry 3

I had an okay day. But then my friend checked in on me, encouraged me, and loved me even though I was not in my most lovable state. She is the reason today went from really hard to okay. Two of my aunts also checked in on me today. One sent a pair of sunshine earrings to brighten my day and the other checked in on my heart and emotions. Both meant so much as I struggled with this jealousy over addiction.

Journal Entry 4

I was feeling isolated, but then I realized that yesterday a friend reached out to Skype and another friend called to check in. My perspective is flawed. I'm loved and valued. God is good, and it is going to be a good day.

I think I want someone to know what's going on and see how strong I'm being (prideful I know, but true.) I want some sort of validation. However, that means I need to let people in. God has been providing so much reassurance and compassion, why can't I be a glass full instead of assuming it's always running dry? Lord help me.

Journal Entry 5

How lucky am I to have so many people reach out to me today? I've never been open or vulnerable, but I was simply honest about not being okay, and WOW, God used so many people to comfort me. Thank you, Lord!

"The times we most need to be surrounded by love and friends are the same times we tend to be the most unlovable," as someone once said.

Journal Entry 6

I feel like page after page of life keeps turning and I'm almost numb to it as this has become my new normal. However, I'm excited to go on a hike tomorrow and I'm grateful for so many blessings God has given me. Things could be so much worse. Right now, it's mainly a case of "could be's" and not to discount those, because there's a big difference between having a healthy sister and having a sister who wants to kill herself. I don't think it's irrational to be concerned about that, but God is in control, and I need to remember that other people are currently going through struggles as well. I'm fearful, but working to fully trust God. Also, I'm really, really tired.

Journal Entry 7

I finally posted on a Facebook page for siblings of alcoholics. I think what surprises me the most is how "normal" everyone is. Everyone in the group has classic Facebook pictures and if you creep on any of our pages you would never know the deep, heart-breaking conversations we have on our page. A deep, dark world all of us are forced to live in because of alcohol. I know I've said it before, but I am so comforted that other people understand me and can empathize. At the same time, it's heartbreaking that so, so many people are in this same situation.

Journal Entry 8

I really wish there was an Al-Anon meeting tonight. There was one this morning, but I had a work training that conflicted with the time. I miss having people who understand the deep pains addiction has inflicted on me. I wonder if it's bad to want other people to know the same pain as me. I like to think I only like commiserating since we're both suffering regardless.

Would I be able to survive if no one understood me? Then again, no one ever really understands another. We're like snowflakes, each of us unique yet easily blended into a snowball. Sure, we all have a similar quality of sharing that ball, but that doesn't negate the uniqueness and individuality of our prior attributes.

14

Revelations and Lessons Learned

LESSON 1

I've come to the conclusion that just like I can't take my sister's recovery away from her, I also can't take my parents' acceptance away from them. The only way people get to a point where they are able to set boundaries healthily is if they come to that decision on their own. Unfortunately, that typically results from repetitive hurt. However, that's what led me to my boundary . . . how easy it is to forget that my counselor told me for months to set a boundary, but it was without talking to her, on my own time, that I finally decided to implement one. It's the same for my parents, of course, it's not going to do any good for me to continually tell them what I think is best. What matters is how they comprehend and realize things for themselves. Sadly, that means they have many heartbreaks ahead, but that also means the weight is off my shoulders. I can only control my healing, it's up to everyone else to control how they live their lives.

LESSON 2

I've realized that in order to move on in life I need to be able to forgive myself for what has happened to me. I always think of events as something I caused or situations that could have been avoided if I were somehow better. Deep down I assume if I had been a better sister, if only I had paid more attention and realized things sooner then Amber could have gotten help. If only I wasn't so easily hurt by her words, then I could have been strong enough to take the pressure off my parents and talk her down from her mental breakdowns. I think that's part of why I'm type A. I assume if I can be early enough or thoroughly prepared for situations, then I can avoid the follies of life. As long as I do enough, then I can control the messy things around me. One of the hardest things about this ordeal has been learning that I am not in control of anything and, just like I need to forgive others, I need to equally forgive myself. And that is where God comes in, because I sure can't do that on my own.

LESSON 3

"Don't blame a clown for acting like a clown. Ask yourself why you keep going to the circus."[1]

I need to take some responsibility in all of this. Amber isn't going to change that she's an alcoholic and yes, that sucks, but I can choose to not attend the circus. I need to be okay with missing the trapeze artists and fun food. Because if I'm willing to miss the good parts, I can also avoid the bad.

LESSON 4

God has shown me that asking for help is a beautiful thing. There is a point where suffering is only for our own pride and as a result, the only person who gets hurt is yourself. It took being fully broken

---

1. Nielsen, "Don't Blame a Clown."

down before I finally turned over my daily life to Christ. If I was humbler or cared less about what others thought, maybe I would have sought help sooner, and it's ironic that even now, knowing better, I wait until my breaking point to reach out. I insist on suffering in silence because I'm worried about burdening others and having people think I'm weak. When, ironically, as a Christian I know I'm weak. After all, isn't that the whole point? I'm weak because God is strong. I don't have to carry this around because I don't have to have strength. God powerfully works in me and as a result, I know that he will carry any burden that I am willing to give to him. Man, oh man, what a beautiful reality.

LESSON 5

I'm realizing that I can both be angered at the ordeals Amber has had to go through and angry that she is an addict. I don't have to choose one side or the other. I can literally just saturate in anger over both. Maybe the mixture creates a new marinade that totally revolutionizes what I thought was normal. Someone once told me, "If she could do better, she would." This whole time I've been holding a grudge as if she purposefully gets drunk just to spite me and make my life hard. It's not fair to take all the many aspects of anger out on one particular person.

LESSON 6

Having these crazy, conflicting emotions is not changing anything in my situation. Therefore, it's okay to wrestle and be confused about my thoughts without totally understanding the nuances. I don't need to prioritize figuring it out because there's no need to have all the answers. In a world as crazy and unpredictable as things are, it's fair to want some certainty in life, but I don't think I truly want to spend my mental energy or time on that task. If it does end up being important then I can focus on it at that point. This, among other things, has been such a beautiful perspective to have. It's such a relief to not have the expectations for my thoughts that I was pressuring myself with.

LESSON 7

Everyone is going through intense struggles behind the scenes, just because my struggles are closer in proximity doesn't mean they are any greater. They simply look larger because they are the hills standing next to me versus the distant mountains that look like little peaks.

LESSON 8

I went to church tonight and we talked about letting people into our families as a part of grace and love. It made me think about how there are always opposite forces. If there is a positive, then a negative must exist. So, since you can add to a family, in theory, you should be able to redefine your unit and subtract as well. I talked with one of the pastors about this afterward and he had some really good advice. He talked about it being a spectrum of forgiveness, a thin line, then codependency. I've continually struggled with knowing I forgive Amber, but the act of letting her back in my life has time and time again shown to be incredibly hurtful to me and without benefit to the relationship. It's so relieving to think that my boundaries are actually protecting her as much as they are me. The fact that there's a line telling her actions have consequences isn't bad. I'm not saying I never want to see her, but I am enforcing that I am also a valuable and loved human who deserves respect. It's okay to set boundaries. Siblings are important too.

LESSON 9

I have realized that getting better and being at my destination are not mutually exclusive. I was so upset that I had failed to make progress in my Al-Anon program because I wasn't doing okay emotionally, but I later realized that both could be true. I may not be totally okay, but that doesn't mean I'm as messed up as I was a few months ago. I can still make progress and not be an expert, just like I can advance in sporting ranks and not be in the Olympics. In the same way, I can love my sister and still struggle with aspects of her life.

LESSON 10

If nothing else comes out of this trial, it will still be worth it because of the people I've been able to connect with and talk to about Al-Anon. I have been to so many clinical environments where the clinicians have never heard about this amazing resource. There are so many patients who will benefit from hearing they are not alone. I hope that with this life experience, I can at least share the resources that I've been introduced to. The resources that have so deeply impacted my life.

LESSON 11

As I was going through journals, I realized I was abbreviating Amber's name as either A or writing her name as amber. I think subconsciously I was minimizing her to justify how I could be so distant and create such a deep space between us. Almost a way to prepare myself for the next hurtful comment or painful situation. I was objectifying her to attempt to lessen the pain. One night at Al-Anon, someone mentioned that "the first step in a genocide is being able to objectify an individual." Something about that rocked me to my core and changed how I looked at everyone around me, including Amber. I went back and changed each of the times I had written her name in any sort of abbreviation. Sometimes it genuinely is the small acts we do that have great impacts.

LESSON 12

Addiction has made my life do a complete about-face from the path I thought I'd be on five years ago, but it hasn't changed ingrained characteristics in me. Really what it has done is acted like a sickness on my body. It has made me aware of flaws I was overlooking. It has revealed cracks that, while complicated by addiction, were present before.

Conclusion

So, what makes my story special? Absolutely nothing. My story is simply a single example of so many lives hurt by addiction. I don't know the ending of my story but, for right now, my sister and I are at a place of peace and for today that's enough. We don't have to be best friends, at least not at this moment. We can both coexist as adults and as long as neither of us is hurting the other, it's okay to give our wounds time to heal. I have hope that one day our relationship will mend to a point that we can both be the best versions of ourselves. If that means our current relationship is the final destination then I'm at peace, but if I can grow and love better by continuing to learn from my sister and addressing past hurts, then that's the road I want to be on.

I've spent so much time focusing on the pain that was caused by my family. Very rarely have I considered that God allowed me to be healthy so that I could help those who are hurting in my family. Asking for help is arguably twice as hard as being the one who has been hurt by the acts. I'm lucky to simply need to forgive. It might not be the same for everyone, but I have a feeling my pride would make it a lot harder for me to make amends as an addict versus a loved one. I don't know how my heart would handle knowing the deep pain if I struggled with addiction. I'm so grateful to be healthy. It turns into a question of how can I bless Amber and give thanks for my luck of being born into her family?

Epilogue
Healing

SUMMARY

I almost didn't add this section, partially because there are years of journals and healing that have occurred since the editing process began. It looks like I skipped to a place of healing, whereas there could be an entire additional book of learning and lessons that happened prior to this point. Furthermore, it took years before I could make it through a full editing session of this book without having extreme anger and depression for the following weeks. So many memories that I had blocked out were relived and, for the first time, partially processed. The pain was intense and the emotions unbearable at times. There were many days I debated if it was actually worth doing, or if it was better to just leave the past in the past and continue trying to pretend it never happened. Another reason I debated adding this section is the mindset I had when I was suffering. I wasn't looking for a story with a happy ending. I hated that all the books I read on addiction had happy endings where the addict got sober and the family started to heal. This isn't always the case, and I want to affirm the stories that don't have that conclusion. I wanted desperately to hear a story where the family members were fine despite the alcoholic not being okay. I wanted someone to empathize with the emotions I was dealing with. However, it would be a fabrication to say I am still as broken as I was years ago. There are still days that overwhelm me. However, for the most part, God has allowed me to begin healing and to see some of the beautiful doors he has opened because of this trial. *I can't be sure that my family's story of addiction will have a happy ending, but I can be sure to not let my family's addiction define my story.* Instead, it can be a situation that helps me become the person I was created to be.

JOURNALS

Journal Entry 1

It's crazy to realize I can process and handle small inconveniences without them completely destroying me. My life isn't dangling on a thread just waiting to unravel. It's both exhausting and thrilling to have some control over what happens.

Maybe it's a good thing that so many thoughts and feelings are pouring over me and forcing me to think about the past. I block out so many traumas and just assume my core being will erase the pain as time moves on. But nothing is totally erased. With therapy and help, one can move on and lessen the pain, but all marks remain a part of what created us to be in our present state. I'm hopeful to unpack some of my deep-rooted scars with my therapist over the next few months. Dealing with trauma is exhausting, but necessary.

Journal Entry 2

I'm okay. I took a walk around my past neighborhood where I took so many tearful runs. The same streets where I used to do sprints to try and physically wear myself out because I was so overstimulated and overwhelmed that I needed something to allow me to slow down enough to focus. I rarely ran for fun during those days, it was always a time to break me out of whatever tragedy was currently happening. It was my sanity during each catastrophe. It felt miraculous today to walk along those same paths and be content to soak in the sunshine and gentle breeze. I was fully at peace and that's a place I wasn't sure I would ever get to. God is so good! I am genuinely okay and no matter what trial or tragedy comes next, God will always be there to support me until I am okay again.

Journal Entry 3

I'm back at the zoo, it's been a few years and the monkey creature I saw before has fully grown into its own being while the mom now has a new baby. I also found that these creatures are called Mandrills. The mom has a firm grip and now it makes sense. Her new baby is three weeks old and jumping all over the place. The baby is trying to get free while simultaneously she's so small that she could be stepped on at any moment. Her features are delicate and fresh. She has an adventurous light in her eyes, but her brain needs some time to develop. Anytime another Mandrill comes close, the mom immediately grabs the baby and moves to an open area where the baby can jump around safely. Intermittently, the mom will give the baby some breast milk, and always the mom protects the baby from the outside environment. Meanwhile, the dad sits on an elevated surface and keeps guard over both the initial child who is now a few years old and this new baby. The Mandrill from a few years ago seems to have turned out quite well despite my concerns. Maybe the parents know best after all. Maybe I don't have it all figured out, and that's okay.

Journal Entry 4

I can't remember the last time I felt like this. Have I ever? Have I ever desired so deeply to lean forward to the future rather than relax back into the potential past? Maybe this is what happens when you work through things, it hurts like hell and breaks you to pieces, but then, you look around and life looks appealing. The pain is there for sure, but it's the dark before the morning. Ironically, I'm mourning to try and get to the morning. I see hope. I see potential. I see the ability to help others and the idea of going on adventures and journeying through life makes me light up. What a beautiful life I live.

I want to live. I want to love. I want to experience all those crazy, weird emotions that one can't fully put into words. I know it will be hard, there will be days I won't be able to get out of bed. But I want to see what comes next. I feel like that old book that sat forever on my bookshelf. I finally read it after so many years of not being able to get engaged. Eventually, I committed and, as a result, I became so fascinated that it was hard to put down. It was truly a gem when I gave it the time it needed. I think that's how I am now. I have finally given my wounds the time they needed to heal and have become disciplined at facing my past and focusing on growing healthier each day. I have decided that life is a beautiful thing. There will be slow times, fast times, crazy times, and all sorts of memories in between. Through it all, I can't wait to see where those tales take my story.

Bibliography

Beaumont, Gabrielle, dir. "Who Knew." Season 2, episode 4 of *7th Heaven*, written by Greg Plageman. Spelling Entertainment, air date Oct. 6, 1997.

Brian & Jenn Johnson. "You're Gonna Be OK." Track 9 on *After All These Years*, written by Jenn Johnson et al., produced by Jason Ingram and Paul Mabury. Bethel Music, 2017.

Cardillo, Erin, and Richard Keith, creators. *Life Sentence*. In Good Company, Doozer, CBS, and Warner Bros., 2018.

Cassavetes, Nick, dir. *My Sister's Keeper*. New Line Cinema and Curmudgeon Films, 2009.

Frederiksen, Lisa. "Sober Child with an Addicted Sibling." Breaking the Cycles, Feb. 14, 2016. https://www.breakingthecycles.com/2016/02/14/sober-child-with-an-addicted-sibling/.

Lusko, Levi. *Through the Eyes of a Lion: Facing Impossible Pain, Finding Incredible Power*. Carol Stream, IL: Tyndale House, 2015.

McGee, Robert S. *The Search for Significance: Seeing Your True Worth Through God's Eyes*. Rev. ed. Nashville: Thomas Nelson, 2003.

McGowan, Robert F., dir. *The Kid from Borneo*. Hal Roach Studios and Metro-Goldwyn-Mayer, 1933.

Nielsen, Dan. "Don't Blame a Clown for Acting Like a Clown." DanNielsen, Mar. 7, 2019. https://dannielsen.com/2019/03/07/dont-blame-a-clown-for-acting-like-a-clown/.

Schwartz, Josh, and Stephanie Savage, creators. *Gossip Girl*. Warner Bros. and Alloy Entertainment, 2007–2012.

Sherman-Palladino, Amy, creator. *Gilmore Girls*. Dorothy Parker Drank Here, Hofflund/Polone, and Warner Bros., 2000–2006.

Stanzler, Wendey, dir. "Deny, Deny, Deny." Season 2, episode 4 of *Grey's Anatomy*, written by Zoanne Clack. ABC Studios, air date Oct. 16, 2005.

Tenth Avenue North. "Worn." Track 3 on *Struggle*, written by Mike Donehey et al., produced by Jason Ingram. Reunion, 2012.

Wilson, William G. *Alcoholics Anonymous: The Story of How Many Thousands of Men and Women Have Recovered from Alcoholism.* 4th ed. New York: Alcoholics Anonymous Word Services, 2001.

Zamm, Alex, dir. *A Christmas Prince.* MPCA, 2017.